D0057192

ETHICS

101

JOHN C. MAXWELL

ETHICS

101

WHAT EVERY LEADER NEEDS TO KNOW

CENTER
STREET

NEW YORK   BOSTON   NASHVILLE

Scriptures noted NKJV are taken from the NEW KING JAMES VER-SION. Copyright © 1979, 1980, 1982, Thomas Nelson, Inc., Publishers.

Scriptures noted NIV are taken from the HOLY BIBLE: NEW INTER-NATIONAL VERSION®. Copyright © 1973, 1978, 1984 by International Bible Society. Used by permission of Zondervan Publishing House. All rights reserved.

Scriptures noted NASB are taken from the New American Standard Bible®, Copyright © 1960, 1962, 1963, 1968, 1972, 1975, 1977, 1995 by The Lockman Foundation. Used by permission.

Scriptures noted The Message are taken from *The Message: The New Testament in Contemporary English*. Copyright © 1993 by Eugene H. Peterson.

Center Street

Warner Books

Time Warner Book Group
1271 Avenue of the Americas, New York, NY 10020
Visit our web site at the www.twbookmark.com.

Center Street and the Center Street logo are registered trademarks of Time Warner Book Group Inc.

Printed in the United States of America

Originally published as *There's No Such Thing as "Business" Ethics*. First Center Street Edition: May 2005

10 9 8 7 6 5 4 3 2 1

ISBN: 0-446-57809-6
LCCN: 2004115129

This book is dedicated to you
for your commitment to making ethical
decisions and living an ethical life. Doing the
right thing may not always be easy—
but it is always right.

CONTENTS

ACKNOWLEDGMENTS

I'd like to say thank you to:

Charlie Wetzel, my writer;

Kathie Wheat, my researcher;

Stephanie Wetzel, who proofs and edits each chapter;

and Linda Eggers, my assistant.

PREFACE

In the summer of 2002, I went to dinner in New York with Laurence J. Kirshbaum, the chairman and CEO of the AOL Time Warner Book Group. As we chatted, at one point in the conversation he looked at me and said, "You know, John, I think you would be the perfect person to do this: What would you think about writing a book on business ethics?"

"There's no such thing," I answered.

"What?" He looked a little surprised by my remark. "What do you mean?" he asked.

"There's no such thing as business ethics—there's only ethics. People try to use one set of ethics for their professional life, another for their spiritual life, and still another at home with their family. That gets them into trouble. Ethics is ethics. If you desire to be ethical, you live it by one standard across the board."

That's the heart of *Ethics 101*. Educators, philosophers, theologians, and lawyers have taken what really is a simple matter and made it very confusing. Living an ethical life may not always be easy, but it need not be complicated. *This book's goal is to help you find the way to live and work ethically and also achieve greater success.*

1

Whatever Happened to Business Ethics?

HOW WOULD YOU DESCRIBE THE STATE OF ETHICS IN BUSINESS today? Wonderful? Rock solid? No, I think most people are disgusted with it. They are sick of dishonesty and unethical dealings.

What is your reaction to the following names: Enron, Dennis Kozlowski, WorldCom, Adelphia Communications? At the least, it's probably a feeling of unsettledness. If you owned stock affected by the ethical scandals associated with these names, you are probably outraged!

UC Berkeley accounting professor Brett Trueman, who teaches at the Haas School of Business, remarked, "This is why the market keeps going down every day—investors don't know who to trust. As these things come out, it just continues to build."[1]

Of course, the ethical problems we're seeing aren't limited to just the business world. The public was horrified by the recently revealed abuses that occurred in the Catholic Church and how the incidents were covered up. Many were surprised by reports that Pulitzer prize–winning history professor Stephen Ambrose had plagiarized passages from historian Thomas Childers for his book *The Wild Blue*.[2] And those who watched the 2002 Winter Olympic Games in Salt Lake City were outraged when a figure-skating judge claimed that her decision had been coerced, altering the outcome of the pairs competition.[3] Ethical lapses are everywhere.

When pollster George Barna asked people whether they had "complete confidence" that leaders from various professions would "consistently make job-related decisions that are morally appropriate," the results were abysmal:[4]

Type of Leader	Percent Who Hold the Public's Complete Confidence
Executives of Large Corporations	3%
Elected Government Officials	3%
Film & TV Producers, Directors & Writers	3%
News Reporters & Journalists	5%
Small Business Owners	8%
Ministers, Priests & Clergy	11%
Teachers	14%

It's revealing that even regarding the most trusted leaders (teachers), six out of seven people are unwilling to give them their complete trust.

THE ETHICAL DILEMMA

Our disgust is now turning to discussion. People want to know: *Why* is ethics in such a terrible state? Although there are many possible responses to that question, I believe when people make unethical choices, they do so for one of three reasons:

1. We Do What's Most Convenient

An ethical dilemma can be defined as an undesirable or unpleasant choice relating to a moral principle or practice. What do we do in such situations? Do we do the easy thing or the right thing? For example, what should I do when a clerk gives me too much change? What should I say when a convenient lie can cover a mistake? How far should I go in my promises to win a client?

AN ETHICAL DILEMMA CAN BE DEFINED AS AN UNDESIRABLE OR UNPLEASANT CHOICE RELATING TO A MORAL PRINCIPLE OR PRACTICE.

As human beings, we seem prone to failing personal ethics tests. Why do we do something even when we know it's wrong? Do we cheat because we think we won't get caught? Do we give ourselves permission to cut corners because we rationalize that it's just one time? Is this our way of dealing with pressure?

2. *We Do What We Must to Win*

I think most people are like me: I hate losing! Businesspeople in particular desire to win through achievement and success. But many think they have to choose between being ethical and winning. The *Atlanta Business Chronicle* reports that a group of executives came together recently at a leading company in Atlanta to brainstorm ideas for a three-day national conference to be attended by several thousand sales employees. As the team shared ideas for different sessions, a senior vice president of the corporation enthusiastically suggested, "Why don't we do a piece on ethics?"

It was as if someone had died. The room went silent. An awkward moment later, the discussion continued as if the vice president had never uttered a word. She was so taken aback by everyone's reaction, she simply let the idea drop.

Later that day, she happened to run into the company's CEO. She recounted to him her belief that the subject of ethics should be addressed at the conference. She expected him to agree wholeheartedly. Instead he replied, "I'm sure everyone agrees that's an important issue. But there's a time and a place for everything. The sales meeting is supposed to be upbeat and motivational. And ethics is such a negative subject."[5]

That CEO isn't alone in his opinion of ethics. Many people believe that embracing ethics would limit their options,

---

MANY PEOPLE BELIEVE THAT EMBRACING ETHICS WOULD LIMIT
THEIR OPTIONS, THEIR OPPORTUNITIES, THEIR VERY ABILITY
TO SUCCEED IN BUSINESS.

---

their opportunities, their very ability to succeed in business. It's the old suspicion that good guys finish last. They agree with Harvard history professor Henry Adams, who stated, "Morality is a private and costly luxury." Ironically, in today's culture of high debt and me-first living, ethics may be the *only* luxury some people are choosing to live without!

If I believe that I have only two choices: (1) to win by doing whatever it takes, even if it's unethical; or (2) to have ethics and lose—I'm faced with a real moral dilemma. Few people set out with the desire to be dishonest, but nobody wants to lose.

3. We Rationalize Our Choices with Relativism

Many people choose to deal with such no-win situations by deciding what's right in the moment, according to their circumstances. That's an idea that gained legitimacy in the early 1960s when Dr. Joseph Fletcher, dean of St. Paul's Cathedral in Cincinnati, Ohio, published a book called *Situation Ethics.*[6] In it he said that love was the only viable standard for determining right from wrong. The Executive Leadership Foundation states,

> According to Fletcher, right is determined by the situation, and love can justify anything—lying, cheating, stealing . . . even murder. This philosophy spread rapidly throughout the theological and educational worlds. . . . Since the 1960s, situational ethics has become the norm for social behavior. After spreading rapidly through the worlds of education, religion, and

government, it has penetrated a new area—the business world. The result is our ethical situation today.[7]

The result is ethical chaos. Everyone has his own standards, which change from situation to situation. And that stance is encouraged. A course entitled "The Ethics of Corporate Management," offered at the University of Michigan, says in its description, "This course is not concerned with the personal moral issues of honesty and truthfulness. It is assumed that the students at this university have already *formed their own standards on these issues.*"[8]

So whatever anyone wants to use as the standard is okay. Making matters worse is people's natural inclination to be easy on themselves, judging themselves according to their *good intentions*—while holding others to a higher standard and judging them by their *worst actions*. Where once our decisions were based on ethics, now ethics are based on our decisions. If it's good for me, then it's good. Where is this trend likely to end?

A CHANGE IN THE WIND

Fortunately, there is an increasing desire for ethical dealing in business. Executive recruiters Heidrick and Struggles state, "In a new era for business, CEOs face a new mandate. Glamour and glitz are out. Transparency—in terms of ethics, values, and goals—is in."[9] My friend Bruce Dingman, president of management consulting firm R. W. Dingman, agrees. He recently sent me an e-mail:

Thought you might like to know what we are seeing in the marketplace. Changes in corporate values or strategies are often reflected in what our clients tell us they now seek in candidates. . . . Yes, they still want key executives who can make the company money, are willing to make tough decisions, and fit the management team, but now there is a stronger concern for integrity, not playing it quite as close to the edge, and taking a somewhat longer view in strategies and the setting of more realistic, more conservative goals.

And Jeremy Farmer, a seasoned recruiter at Bank One in Chicago, says that he and his colleagues are taking ethics into greater account when looking for potential employees: "We're asking the ethics-type questions, and we're doing behavioral interviewing."[10]

It's good to know that there is a desire for change regarding ethics in our culture. The bad news is that most people don't know how to make that transition. Their situation is like that of a group of passengers in a corny joke I heard many years ago. The people were on an airplane during a cross-country flight. About two hours into their journey they heard a voice say over the loudspeaker, "This is your pilot. We are currently cruising at 35,000 feet at an air speed of 700 knots. We have some bad news and some good news. The bad news is we're lost. The good news is we're making excellent time."

SOME CURRENT MARKETPLACE SOLUTIONS

If you look at what's happening in the marketplace, you'll see that even though we desire honesty and plain dealing, we're still not winning the battle of ethics. Take a look at how people in our culture are currently trying to address the problem. They . . .

Outsource Ethics Instruction

According to Joan Ryan, columnist for the *San Francisco Chronicle,* companies are hiring firms to offer on-line ethics classes and engaging consultants to produce huge ethics manuals that Ryan says "often read like tax codes, complete with loopholes and fine print." It's not helping. Worst of all, the desire of such companies often isn't to make their businesses more ethical. Ryan states, "It's about evading punishment. Under federal guidelines, companies that have ethics programs are eligible for reduced fines if convicted of wrongdoing."[11]

Perform an Ethical Flea Dip

Another approach is to "treat" ethical offenders when caught. Management consultant Frank J. Navran calls that an "ethical flea dip."[12] The problem with this approach is that it is as effective as a flea dip when a dog's environment isn't changed. The fleas come right back. If the environment—the systems and goals—of an organization encourage and reward unethical behavior, then merely addressing individual employees' actions will not improve the situation.

Rely on the Law

Some companies have given up entirely on trying to figure out what's ethical and are instead using what's legal as their standard for decision making. The result is moral bankruptcy. When Kevin Rollins, president of the Dell Computer Corporation, was asked about the role of ethics in business, he paraphrased Russian dissident Aleksandr Solzhenitsyn, who said, "I've lived my life in a society where there was no rule of law. And that's a terrible existence. But a society where the rule of law is the only standard of ethical behavior is equally bad." Rollins asserts, "Solzhenitsyn said that if the United States only aspires to a legal standard of moral excellence, we will have missed the point. Man can do better. I thought that was a nice comment on the ethics of companies that say, 'Well, legally, it was just fine.' We believe you have to aspire to something higher than what's legal. Is what you're doing right?"[13]

THIS TIME IT'S PERSONAL

One of our problems is that ethics is never a business issue or a social issue or a political issue. It is always a personal issue. People say they want integrity. But at the same time, ironically, studies indicate that the majority of people don't always act with the kind of integrity they request from others. Among college students, 84 percent believe the United States is experiencing a business crisis, and 77 percent believe CEOs should be held responsible for it. However, 59 percent of those same students admit to having cheated

> THE SAME PERSON WHO CHEATS ON HIS TAXES OR STEALS
> OFFICE SUPPLIES WANTS HONESTY AND INTEGRITY FROM THE
> CORPORATION WHOSE STOCK HE BUYS, THE POLITICIAN HE
> VOTES FOR, AND THE CLIENT HE DEALS WITH IN HIS
> OWN BUSINESS.

on a test.[14] In the workplace, 43 percent of people admit to having engaged in at least one unethical act in the last year, and 75 percent have observed such an act and done nothing about it.[15] The same person who cheats on his taxes or steals office supplies wants honesty and integrity from the corporation whose stock he buys, the politician he votes for, and the client he deals with in his own business.

It's easy to *discuss* ethics and even easier to be *disgusted* with people who fail the ethics test—especially when we have been violated by the wrongdoing of others. It's harder to make ethical choices in our own lives. When we are faced with unpleasant choices, what are we going to do? In the 1980s, former President Ronald Reagan quipped that when it comes to the economy, it's a recession when your neighbor loses his job, but it's a depression when you lose yours! Ethics is similar. It's always harder when I'm the one having to make the choice.

THE BOTTOM LINE ON ETHICS

I want to be ethical, and I believe that you do too. Furthermore, I know it really is possible to do what's right *and* succeed in business. In fact, according to the Ethics Resource Center in Washington, D.C., companies that are dedicated to doing the right thing, have a written commitment to social responsibility, and act on it consistently are more profitable than those who don't. James Burke, chairman of Johnson and Johnson, says, "If you invested $30,000 in a composite of the Dow Jones thirty years ago, it would be worth $134,000 today. If you had put that $30,000 into these [socially and ethically responsible] firms—$2,000 into each of the fifteen [in the study]—it would now be worth over $1 million."[16]

COMPANIES THAT ARE DEDICATED TO DOING THE RIGHT THING, HAVE A WRITTEN COMMITMENT TO SOCIAL RESPONSIBILITY, AND ACT ON IT CONSISTENTLY ARE MORE PROFITABLE THAN THOSE WHO DON'T.

If you embrace ethical behavior, will it automatically make you rich and successful? Of course not. Can it pave the way for you to become successful? Absolutely! *Ethics + Competence* is a winning equation. In contrast, people who continually attempt to test the edge of ethics inevitably go over that edge. Shortcuts never pay off in the long run. It may be possible to fool people for a season, but in the long haul, their deeds will catch up with them because the truth does come out. In the short term, behaving ethically may look like a loss (just as one *can temporarily appear to win* by being unethical). However, in the long term, people *always lose* when they live without ethics. Have you ever met anyone who lived a life of shortcuts, deception, and cheating who finished well?

King Solomon of ancient Israel, reputed to be the wisest man who ever lived, said it this way:

The ways of right-living people glow with light;
　the longer they live, the brighter they shine.
But the road of wrongdoing gets darker and darker—
　travelers can't see a thing; they fall flat on their faces.[17]

U.S. representative and educational rights advocate Jabez L. M. Curry observed, "A state to prosper must be built on foundations of a moral character, and this character is the principal element of its strength, and the only guaranty of its permanence and prosperity." The same can be said of a business. Or of a family. Or of any endeavor you wish to see thrive and endure. However, that foundation cannot be built by the organization as a whole. It must be built beginning with each individual. And it must be done in the face of continuous pressure to perform at the expense of doing the right thing.

Let's go back to basics. How do you know what's right? How do you navigate even the most difficult of pressure-filled situations? Where can you find a standard that will work in every situation—a guide that will help you to sleep well at night, prosper in business, improve your marriage, and have confidence that you're doing all you can every time? I offer what I believe to be the best answer to those questions in the next chapter.

2

Why This Rule Is Golden

HOW DO YOU RATE YOURSELF WHEN IT COMES TO ETHICS? German-born industrial relations lecturer and clergyman William J. H. Boetcker observed, "Men must be honest with themselves before they can be honest with others. A man who is not honest with himself presents a hopeless case."[1] I believe all people can be categorized using the following five statements.

1. I am always ethical.
2. I am mostly ethical.
3. I am somewhat ethical.
4. I am seldom ethical.
5. I am never ethical.

Which one best applies to you? How would you characterize yourself? Pause to reflect. Then go ahead and put a check mark next to the statement that best describes you.

ETHICS MATTERS

Now that you've given that some thought, here are some observations I want to share with you related to how people look at ethics:

1. The majority of people place themselves in the first or second category. Most of us try to be ethical most of the time.

2. Most people who put themselves in the second category do so because of personal convenience. Conflict is inconvenient. Practicing discipline is inconvenient. Losing is inconvenient. Paying a high price for success is inconvenient. Some people in category 2 are there because they don't want to deal with those inconveniences.

3. Most people think that being "mostly ethical" is fine—unless they are on the losing end of someone else's lapse in ethics.

4. One rule can help people move from "mostly ethical" to "always ethical" and close the gap between the first two categories.

In the preface of this book, I mentioned that educators, philosophers, theologians, and lawyers have made ethics an overly complex subject. Most people have been influenced by the view of those "experts." To see evidence of that fact, pay attention to your reaction to what I'm about to tell you: I believe you will be able to use one guideline to govern all your ethical decision making. It's based on the Golden Rule.

I BELIEVE YOU WILL BE ABLE TO USE ONE GUIDELINE TO GOVERN ALL YOUR ETHICAL DECISION MAKING. IT'S BASED ON THE GOLDEN RULE.

Did you scoff? Are you skeptical? Are you considering dismissing my assertion? If you are, then you may be caught in the quagmire of modern thinking on ethics. I'd like to ask you to bear with me as I explain the thesis of this book, which is:

Asking the question "How would I like to be treated
in this situation?" is an integrity guideline for
any situation.

Now, let me explain why I believe the Golden Rule can become your North Star when it comes to ethical navigation.

ONE RULE FOR EVERYONE

One of the people who has mentored me in leadership is business consultant Fred Smith Sr. One day at lunch more than a decade ago, we got to talking about ethics, and we discussed the Golden Rule. "You know," Fred said, "a version of the Golden Rule exists in just about every culture."

That statement always stuck with me. In America's current relativistic culture—where everyone wants to use different standards and where every situation is supposed to require its own code of conduct—it's promising to hope that people from every culture desiring to live ethically can agree on one standard. Take a look at the results of some research that shows how many variations on the Golden Rule exist:

Christianity: "Whatever you want men to do to you, do also to them."[2]

Islam: "No one of you is a believer until he loves for his neighbor what he loves for himself."[3]

Judaism: "What is hateful to you, do not do to your fellow man. This is the entire Law; all the rest is commentary."[4]

Buddhism: "Hurt not others with that which pains yourself."[5]

Hinduism: "This is the sum of duty; do naught unto others what you would not have them do unto you."[6]

Zoroastrianism: "Whatever is disagreeable to yourself, do not do unto others."[7]

Confucianism: "What you do not want done to yourself, do not do to others."[8]

Bahai: "And if thine eyes be turned towards justice, choose thou for thy neighbour that which thou choosest for thyself."[9]

Jainism: "A man should wander about treating all creatures as he himself would be treated."[10]

Yoruba Proverb (Nigeria): "One going to take a pointed stick to pinch a baby bird should first try it on himself to feel how it hurts."[11]

THERE ARE REALLY ONLY TWO IMPORTANT POINTS WHEN IT COMES TO ETHICS. THE FIRST IS A STANDARD TO FOLLOW. THE SECOND IS THE WILL TO FOLLOW IT.

It is clear that the Golden Rule cuts across cultural and religious boundaries and is embraced by people from nearly every part of the world. It's the closest thing to a universal guideline for ethics a person can find. There are really only two important points when it comes to ethics. The first is a standard to follow. The second is the will to follow it. The Josephson Institute of Ethics, a nonpartisan, nonprofit organization that exists to improve the ethical quality of society, states it well when they say, "Ethics is about how we meet the challenge of doing the right thing when that will cost more than we want to pay. There are two aspects to ethics: The first involves the ability to discern right from wrong, good from evil, and propriety from impropriety. The second involves the commitment to do what is right, good and proper. Ethics entails action; it is not just a topic to mull or debate."[12]

WHY YOU AND I SHOULD ADOPT THE GOLDEN RULE

I'm not naive. I know that not everyone is looking for a simple, practical, and applicable guideline to live ethically. Some people choose to lie, cheat, steal, and do worse. Others live to mull and debate ideas. (I took classes from

> "ETHICS IS ABOUT HOW WE MEET THE CHALLENGE OF DOING THE RIGHT THING WHEN THAT WILL COST MORE THAN WE WANT TO PAY."
> —THE JOSEPHSON INSTITUTE OF ETHICS

some of them in graduate school!) But people who desire to find a good, honest standard of ethical behavior to live by can find it in the Golden Rule. Here is why I believe that:

1. The Golden Rule Is Accepted by Most People

You already have an idea of how widely accepted the Golden Rule is. But if that isn't enough for you, a case can also be made for the Golden Rule based on common sense. Can you imagine someone saying, "Please treat me worse than I treat you"? No, everyone wants to be treated well. Even people who pursue unhealthy relationships or who engage in destructive behavior don't *desire* or consciously seek bad treatment from others. It is not unreasonable for any person to desire good treatment from others. Nor is it asking too much to expect people to treat others well.

It is very difficult for people to justify demanding better treatment from others than they give. What can they base it on? Wealth? If that's the case, then the person making $100,000 a year who desires good treatment from someone making $25,000 must agree to be treated poorly by those who make $500,000!

What if people based treatment on talent? (That's what some of the divas in the music industry have been known to do, for example.) Should the more talented get better treatment than the less talented? Yes? Okay, then who should treat whom better: Whitney Houston or Yo Yo Ma? Do you determine treatment on the *amount* of natural talent or on what people *do* with their talent? How do you judge something as subjective as talent anyway? And what happens when a person with talent in one area meets some-one with talent in another? Who deserves the better treat-ment: Tiger Woods or Bill Gates?

Or people could base treatment on political affiliation or personally held beliefs. Then members of the other party become inherently inferior, and if someone dis-agrees with your beliefs, they automatically deserve poorer treatment. But what if you later find out that *they* were actually right concerning an issue instead of you? The tables turn.

You can see where this can go. No matter what arbitrary criteria you can think of—whether it's wealth, talent, ideol-ogy, nationality, race, or something else—it cannot be logi-cally supported. It eventually becomes like a game of king of the hill. Did you play that as a kid? One person climbs up onto a hill of dirt and tries to stay there while everyone else tries to knock him off. The only way to win is to be the biggest bully. And even if you *do* win, you get pretty beat up in the process.

One of the first rules in human relations is to seek com-mon ground with others. That's a good guideline whether you are exploring a new friendship, meeting with a client, teaching a student, connecting with children, or arguing with your spouse. Comparing similar experiences and dis-covering shared beliefs can pave the way for successful

THE GOLDEN RULE CAN BE USED TO CREATE COMMON
GROUND WITH ANY REASONABLE PERSON.

relationships. The Golden Rule can be used to create common ground with any reasonable person.

2. The Golden Rule Is Easy to Understand

Former *Saturday Review of Literature* editor Norman Cousins, who taught at UCLA, observed:

> The words "hard" and "soft" are generally used by medical students to describe the contrasting nature of courses. Courses like biochemistry, physics, pharmacology, anatomy, and pathology are anointed with the benediction of "hard," whereas subjects like medical ethics, philosophy, history, and patient-physician relationships tend to labor under the far less auspicious label "soft." . . . [But] a decade or two after graduation there tends to be an inversion. That which was supposed to be hard turns out to be soft, and vice versa. The knowledge base of medicine is constantly changing. . . . But the soft subjects—especially those that have to do with intangibles—turn out to be of enduring value.[13]

Cousins's remark sheds light on a problem with ethics. People often have difficulty getting a handle on the subject because it seems complex and intangible. One of the wonderful things about the Golden Rule is that it makes the intangible tangible. You don't need to know the law. You don't need to explore nuances of philosophy. You simply imagine yourself in the place of another person. Even a small child can get a handle on that. There are no complicated rules and no loopholes.

That's not to say every ethical situation can be solved instantly by using the Golden Rule. Sometimes the hardest part of asking "How would I like to be treated in this situation?" is identifying *who* might be affected by the situation and *how* they might be impacted. But even for complex issues, if a person gives the matter some thought, he or she can almost always figure it out.

3. The Golden Rule Is a Win-Win Philosophy

Have you met people who believe that in order for them to be winners, other people must be made to lose? They see everyone as an enemy who must be crushed. Or they prey on the pain of others in order to win. That seems to be the idea behind a mutual fund that became available in September of 2002. It's called the Vice Fund and is offered by Mutuals.com, Inc. The managers of the fund tout it as an investment in "companies that derive a significant portion of their revenues from products often considered socially irresponsible," primarily in gambling, tobacco, alcohol, and defense weapons, industries they consider to be nearly "recession-proof."[14]

Experts say that such "vice investing" doesn't work and isn't as profitable as investment in "socially responsible" companies.[15] But it's clear even from the name that the appeal of the fund comes from the idea of the investor making money from someone else's weaknesses. I wonder how the fund manager would feel if he discovered people were working hard to exploit his personal flaws for their profit. When you live by the Golden Rule, everybody wins. If I treat you as well as I desire to be treated, you win. If you treat me likewise, I win. Where is the loser in that?

4. The Golden Rule Is a Compass When You Need Direction

The Golden Rule does more than just give people wins. It also has internal value for anyone who practices it. Television commentator Ted Koppel says, "There's harmony and inner peace to be found in following a moral compass that points in the same direction regardless of fashion or trend." In a world with much uncertainty, I think many people are seeking direction. The Golden Rule can provide that. It never changes, even as circumstances do. It gives solid, predictable direction every time it's used. And best of all, it actually *works*.

"THERE'S HARMONY AND INNER PEACE TO BE FOUND IN FOLLOWING A MORAL COMPASS THAT POINTS IN THE SAME DIRECTION REGARDLESS OF FASHION OR TREND."
—TED KOPPEL

THE GOLDEN PLACE TO BE

As I speak to corporations throughout the country, I meet a lot of interesting people and many excellent leaders. While on a book tour in 1998, I met someone who fits in both categories. Jim Blanchard is the CEO of Synovus Financial Corp., a holding company for thirty-eight banks in five states, and 80 percent owner of an electronic payment services provider (called TSYS). The company's Web site states that its name is "a combination of the words *synergy* and *novus—synergy,* meaning the interaction of separate components such that the result is greater than the sum of its parts; and *novus,* which means usually of superior quality and different from the others listed in the same category." The organization possesses more than $18 billion in assets, employs more than nine thousand people, and is a component of the Standard & Poor's 500 index (NYSE: SNV).[16]

If you keep up with business news, you may have heard of Synovus. In 1998, *Fortune* magazine began publishing its list of the 100 Best Companies to Work For in America. In 1999, Synovus was ranked number one! The company has been on that list every year since its inception. (The list that came out in January of 2003 ranked Synovus ninth in the nation.)

As a business owner, I wanted to find out how one went about creating the best company to work for in the United States. So I talked to Jim. He told me that a few years after graduating from law school in 1965, at age twenty-nine, he was selected to head the Columbus Bank and Trust Company. Over the years, he built and expanded the business. But then in the 1990s, he realized that he wanted to make sure the ethical principles and values he had always used personally to conduct business would become part of the culture of the expanding organization. "We needed to institutionalize it, and we needed to enforce it and reinforce it," he said. And that meant making changes—big changes. Many policies that had developed over the years were dismantled, such as the promotion system, salary administration, and review process.

They also initiated what Jim calls a People Development Component, the core of which is a commitment to their workforce. Jim explained,

As leaders of Synovus, we said we were not going to allow a mean-spirited, manipulative, commanding sort of leadership to exist in this company any longer. And we were going to remediate anybody who was like that—if they were willing to try. But if they couldn't or wouldn't change, then we would ask them to go somewhere else.

This is going to be a safe place to work. Employees are not going to be harassed. They are not going to be jerked around—we call it "salute the flag and kick the dog," meaning you say all the right things, but then you go back to your office and just beat up the folks. I stood up in a number of forums and said, "I'm writing you a blank check on this promise, and I want you to present it for payment. And if the check bounces, then you've got no reason to believe anything I tell you ever again."

> "IF WE HAD ONLY ONE RULE IN THIS COMPANY, IT WOULD BE THE GOLDEN RULE. IF WE'VE GOT THAT ONE RIGHT, NO OTHER RULES ARE NECESSARY."—JIM BLANCHARD

Very quickly the light of day shone on the bad leaders. We've had two to three hundred of them transition out in the last six or eight years, because they wouldn't live up to the standard of treating folks right, with respect, admiration, appreciation, consideration. And basically we culminated all of this by saying that if we had only one rule in this company, it would be the Golden Rule. If we've got that one right, no other rules are necessary.[17]

To many people, the Golden Rule sounds like a soft approach to business. But nothing could be farther from the truth. At Synovus, arrogance is not tolerated, but excellence is expected. Jim says, "Our policies are not a cover for lazy, average and mediocre. We're very demanding and competitive, but we don't jerk people around, either."[18] When I asked him about the benefits of a Golden Rule approach to people, he said,

The tangible benefits are lower turnover, fewer EEOC claims, almost a disappearance of any kind of harassment issues. But intangible [benefits are that] you keep your best folks, your young emerging leaders want to stay, and people grow and flourish in an environment where they are not suppressed. So you're getting optimum and maximum growth at the highest level. . . . And when you've got people flourishing everywhere around you, then it's like drafting in a race car. It's pulling other people along and people aspire to achieve and accomplish like they see others doing. Following the Golden Rule is a win-win.[19]

It really is a win for everybody! The Golden Rule is good for employees. It's good for clients. And it's good for investors. According to the Robinson-Humphrey Company, Synovus's stock has generated the second highest return of any stock traded on the New York Stock Exchange during the past twenty years![20] That's the kind of return everyone desires. The Golden Rule really does work. That's Ethics 101.

3

The Golden Rule Begins with You

AUTHOR AND SPEAKER ZIG ZIGLAR RECENTLY SENT A NOTE TO me after listening to a lesson I had done on the leadership of our nation's founding fathers. Zig and I have been good friends for years, and I always enjoy receiving his perspective and wisdom on leadership. Here's what he said:

> I believe the reason we had so many outstanding leaders in the early part of our country's history is the fact that, according to the Thomas Jefferson Research Institute, in the days when the men you were mentioning were growing up, over 90 percent of the educational thrust was of a moral, ethical, religious nature. And yet, by the 1950s the percentage of that same educational thrust was so small it could not be measured. I wonder if that's the reason three million Americans in 1776 produced Washington, Madison, Jefferson, Hamilton, Adams, etc., and why in the year 2002 we have no one to equal the men of that caliber.[1]

A strong moral education, such as Zig identified, empowers a person to make good ethical choices. However, since few people today have received such a foundation, how does one get started? How do you take something as broad as the Golden Rule and make it a part of your everyday thinking? I'm convinced the best way to get started is to think about what *you* want.

HOW DO YOU WANT TO BE TREATED?

I believe that all people, at their core, are very much alike. Talk to individuals of any age, gender, race, or nationality, and they have certain things in common. And once you identify those common characteristics, recognizing them first in yourself and then in others, you hold the key that unlocks the Golden Rule. Here is the short list of things that I believe all human beings have in common when it comes to how they want to be treated:

1. I Want to Be Valued

Did you know that in the American marketplace today, 70 percent of the people who leave their jobs do so because they do not feel valued?[2] That's an indictment of how poorly many businesspeople treat their employees. There isn't a person in the world who doesn't want to be valued

---

IN THE AMERICAN MARKETPLACE TODAY, 70 PERCENT OF THE PEOPLE WHO LEAVE THEIR JOBS DO SO BECAUSE THEY DO NOT FEEL VALUED.

---

by others. Don't you want others to accept you for who you are and show you through their actions that you matter?

One business that excels at valuing its employees is Mission Controls, an Irvine, California, based company that designs and installs automated food and beverage systems. The organization works from contract to contract, so they sometimes experience down periods with relatively little work. Many similar companies simply lay off employees when business slows down. But not Mission Controls. Company founders Craig Nelson, Neal Vaoifi, and Scott Young decided when they started their business that they would personally go without pay before laying off any of their thirty-five employees.

The founders' desire to keep their best people and show that they valued them was a pretty idealistic goal. And their commitment to it was tested the company's first year in existence when they experienced a dry period that lasted eight months. But they stuck to their guns and went without salaries during that entire time.

Mission Controls' founders continue to stick with their commitment. Any time sales drop and cost cutting doesn't save enough, the comptroller of the company makes the call and puts the leaders' salary suspension plan into effect. During that time, employee pay and benefits remain unchanged. Once the company reaches certain thresholds for cash flow and profitability, the executives start to receive a salary again. And in case you were wondering, they are *not* paid retroactively. Nelson observes, "It seems like companies will do whatever they need to in order to turn a profit but at the expense of people."[3] Nelson, Vaoifi, and Young understand the importance of being valued, and they treat their employees in the way they would like to be treated.

Have you ever been made to feel worthless by another person? Maybe a parent told you that you had nothing to offer. Or a boss said that you or your department was nothing but a liability to the company. Or perhaps you've been publicly humiliated. If so, then you know how important it is to be valued by another human being. Encouragement is oxygen for the soul. Deep down, all people want to feel they matter simply for who they are.

Valuing others, not for what they can do but simply because they are human beings, is the foundation of the Golden Rule. If you can learn to think in those terms, then you've taken an important step in making the Golden Rule the ethical guideline for your life.

2. I Want to Be Appreciated

The desire to be loved and valued is perhaps the deepest need of every person. Closely related to that need is our desire to be appreciated for what we can do. Don't you possess a desire to excel and achieve? And don't you want to be appreciated for the skill and effort you bring to your work? Knowing that what you do matters builds your self-confidence and self-worth. The people who work with you and for you possess the same desire, even those who don't show it. Human relations expert and author Donald Laird asserted, "Always help people increase their own self-esteem. Develop your skill in making other people feel important. There is hardly a higher compliment you can pay an individual than helping him to be useful and to find satisfaction in his usefulness."

How can you do that? Begin by letting people know that you appreciate their efforts. Thank them at every opportunity. Give credit to others every time you can. And make it a point to praise people in the presence of those closest to them, such as family members. Broadway producer and entertainment entrepreneur Billy Rose shrewdly observed, "It's hard for a fellow to keep a chip on his shoulder if you allow him to take a bow."

3. I Want to Be Trusted

Victorian writer George MacDonald said, "To be trusted is a greater compliment than to be loved." The Law of Solid Ground in *The 21 Irrefutable Laws of Leadership* states that trust is the foundation of leadership. While that is true, it can also be said that trust is the foundation of *all* good relationships. Good marriages, good business relationships, and good friendships all require trust. If you don't have trust, there can be no open and honest interaction, and the relationship will be only temporary.

Manchester Inc., a consulting firm in Philadelphia, used a survey of more than two hundred companies to discover the best ways to build trust with employees. They found that people who engender trust . . .

"TO BE TRUSTED IS A GREATER COMPLIMENT THAN
TO BE LOVED."—GEORGE MACDONALD

- Maintain integrity.
- Openly communicate vision and values.
- Show respect for employees as equal partners.
- Focus on shared goals rather than personal agendas.
- Do the right thing regardless of personal risk.
- Listen with an open mind.
- Demonstrate compassion.
- Maintain confidences.[4]

While you cannot control whether people give you their trust, you can control your actions toward them. And you can determine to give them *your* trust. Former U.S. Secretary of State Henry L. Stimson remarked, "The chief lesson I have learned in a long life is that the only way you can make a man trustworthy is by trusting him; and the surest way to make him untrustworthy is to distrust him and show your distrust."

It takes a leap of faith to put your trust in another person, especially someone you don't know well. Yet that's what it takes to practice the Golden Rule. As you strive to invest confidence in others in the same way you would like it invested in you, take comfort in the words of Camillo Benso di Cavour, who said, "The man who trusts men will make fewer mistakes than he who distrusts them."

4. I Want to Be Respected

When others trust me, I receive responsibility and authority. When others respect me, it touches something deeper within me. It gives me dignity, and it builds my confidence. Indian general and onetime Olympic athlete Dalip Singh observed, "A man who does not respect his own life and that of others robs himself of his dignity as a human being."

Not long ago I read an article about a young man who, at age twenty-three, went to work as the senior pastor of his first church. He found the experience very intimidating because he was to be the spiritual leader of people who had children and grandchildren older than he was. His story intrigued me because I faced a very similar situation early in my career. How did he handle it? By showing his people respect and asking them to treat him in kind. To make his standard clear to everyone, he shared ten rules for respect that he promised to live by, and he asked his people to do the same. Here are his rules:

1. If you have a problem with me, come to me (privately).
2. If I have a problem with you, I'll come to you (privately).
3. If someone has a problem with me and comes to you, send them to me. (I'll do the same for you.)
4. If someone consistently will not come to me, say, "Let's go see him together. I am sure he will see us about this." (I will do the same for you.)
5. Be careful how you interpret me—I'd rather do that. On matters that are unclear, do not feel pressured to

interpret my feelings or thoughts. It is easy to misinterpret intentions.

6. I will be careful how I interpret you.
7. If it's confidential, don't tell. If you or anyone else comes to me in confidence, I won't tell unless (a) the person is going to harm himself/herself, (b) the person is going to physically harm someone else, (c) a child has been physically or sexually abused. I expect the same from you.
8. I do not read unsigned letters or notes.
9. I do not manipulate; I will not be manipulated; do not let others manipulate you. Do not let others try to manipulate me through you.
10. When in doubt, just say it. If I can answer it without misrepresenting something or breaking a confidence, I will.[5]

Author Arnold Glasow said, "The respect of those you respect is worth more than the applause of the multitude." Most people greatly desire the respect of the people they work for. And when employers give it freely, it creates a very positive working environment. An employer who models that is Mitchell Burman, CEO of the consulting firm Analytics Operations Engineering in Boston. He shows his employees the kind of respect every responsible person desires. The ten consultants he employs are regarded as professionals and treated as partners—which they can eventually become by purchasing shares of stock in the company after working there a year. But even before then, they are allowed to make choices mere employees rarely

---

"THE RESPECT OF THOSE YOU RESPECT IS WORTH MORE THAN
THE APPLAUSE OF THE MULTITUDE."—ARNOLD GLASOW

---

get to make. They choose which projects they work on, when they work, where they work, and even how much vacation they take.

"I judge an employee's value by what they create," says Burman. "It doesn't matter to me where they do it or even if they do it from Timbuktu." His main concern is that each consultant be able to bill at least $100,000 a year and that each dollar billed be divided this way: 30 percent to the one who does the work, 15 percent to the person who sells it, 10 percent to whoever manages it, 5 percent to taxes, 20 percent to overhead, and 20 percent to profit.[6]

The kind of respect employees receive gives them the freedom to perform at their best and the incentive to work with excellence. And not only does it honor the person, but it's good for business. James Howell said, "Respect a man, and he will do the more."

5. I Want to Be Understood

I once read about a group of teachers who conducted a survey of two thousand employers, asking them to identify the last three persons they let go and the reason for it. What the teachers discovered was that in two out of three cases, the employees lost their job because they could not get along with others.

Sometimes people problems are caused by an individual's callousness or indifference. But more often the difficulty comes from a lack of understanding. We can be quick to find fault with others when they don't conform to the patterns or standards we hold. But if we make the effort to get to know them, we often discover that their way isn't the wrong way— it's just a different way. We may find they respond differently because they haven't had the advantages we have. Or we realize they may be reacting to conditions or actions that are beyond their control. Once we get beyond those conditions, we can connect with others emotionally, which is what understanding is really all about. We can't expect people to act like machines. We are all creatures of emotion.

When dealing with others, seek first to understand, then to be understood. That requires an attitude of flexibility and teachability. Theologian Hans Küng observed, "Understanding someone properly involves learning from him, and learning from someone properly involves changing oneself." Understanding other people means extending yourself to them and meeting them on their level, putting the burden of making a connection on yourself, not on them. And it is

---

WHEN DEALING WITH OTHERS, SEEK FIRST TO UNDERSTAND, THEN TO BE UNDERSTOOD.

---

wise to remember the words of inventor Charles Kettering, who said, "There is a great difference between knowing and understanding: You can know a lot about something and not really understand it." The same is true about people.

6. I Do Not Want Others to Take Advantage of Me

When it comes to how others treat me, more than anything else I don't want anyone to take advantage of me. That's really the bottom line regarding ethical behavior. Most of us don't need to sort out complicated philosophical issues or ethical conundrums. If people could construe that I am taking advantage of them (even after I've had a chance to explain my motives) then my actions are probably a bad idea.

In January of 2003, Marvin Bower died. He was the longtime leader of McKinsey & Company, which has been called the founder of professional management consulting. Bower joined the organization in 1933. He became its managing director in 1950 and held that position for seventeen years, then worked as a director and partner until his retirement in 1992. Bower had a profound impact on the company from the time he began working for it. He instilled the value of putting others first. "He insisted that client interests be placed before the firm's," says a company publication, "and that engagements be undertaken only when our value to the client was expected to exceed our fees."[7]

That wasn't just lip service. In the 1950s, Bower was asked by billionaire Howard Hughes to help him with Paramount Pictures. Bower went out to Los Angeles and met with Hughes, and he was received with royal treatment. Hughes himself took him around and even gave Bower a personal tour of the *Spruce Goose,* the wooden plane Hughes built that became the largest winged aircraft ever to have flown. But after examining Paramount's problems and considering Hughes's unorthodox approach to business, Bower concluded that he wouldn't be able to help him. So he declined the offer. Values mattered more to him than money.[8] He would not take advantage of another person. That's the way someone who is guided by the Golden Rule lives!

It would have been easy for Marvin Bower to rationalize taking money from Howard Hughes and giving nothing of value back to him. After all, Hughes was worth billions of

---

IT DOESN'T MATTER WHETHER YOU'RE TALKING ABOUT
LYING TO YOUR NEIGHBOR OR DEFRAUDING A BIG
CORPORATION, ANY ACTION ULTIMATELY IMPACTS
INDIVIDUAL PEOPLE—FOR BETTER OR WORSE.

---

dollars; he would never have missed it. But that's not the point. It doesn't matter whether you're talking about lying to your neighbor or defrauding a big corporation; any action ultimately impacts individual people—for better or worse. And if that action devalues or takes advantage of them, it hurts them in a way we would not like to be hurt.

BACK TO PEOPLE

Some companies in the United States are relearning this lesson. They are rediscovering the value of valuing people, and they are making changes to promote the good treatment of their employees. One such company is HomeBanc, a mortgage company based in Atlanta that employs more than one thousand people. After searching for more than a year and a half (and placing national full-page ads costing more than $50,000), the company found what it was looking for: a chief people officer.

HomeBanc chairman Patrick Flood says, "There's been some significant gaps in character that's been displayed in leadership in corporate and government roles. CEOs have gotten way too full of themselves believing they're the success of the business. The fact is, we play a real role, but the real success are the people who do the heavy lifting—the workers."[9] To help the company remain focused on its people while expanding by 50 percent in two years, they hired Dr. Dwight "Ike" Reighard, a pastor who has spent twenty-eight years working with people. Ike, who happens to be a friend of mine, holds the responsibility of shepherding the company's corporate culture and honing its ethical standards of leadership. It's a perfect fit for him.

And what will he do to help Homebanc continue to put its people first? That's simple. He'll remind everyone to treat others as they want to be treated. When a person has a good sense of how he wants to be treated—with dignity, respect, understanding, and trust—then he can easily figure out how to treat others.

4

Living a 24-Karat-Gold Life

WHEN YOU THINK ABOUT COLLEGE ATHLETICS PROGRAMS IN the U.S., what comes to mind? Fans, alumni, and boosters rabidly screaming for their teams' success? Players more concerned with exploiting their personal privileges on campus than their opponents' weaknesses during games? Coaches with win-at-all-costs attitudes obsessed with obtaining a championship? If that's what you picture, then you need to know about Coach Mark Richt of the University of Georgia.

When Richt was hired by the University of Georgia in December of 2000, he was obviously expected to make a positive impact on the team. Like most men who become head coaches of large NCAA football programs, Richt had a history of success. Despite being only forty years old, he had fifteen years of experience, including seven years at Florida State University as the coordinator of one of the nation's most potent offenses. (While Richt was offensive coordinator, FSU's offense ranked in the top five in the nation five of seven years.) And he turned the University of Georgia's team around quickly. In two seasons, Richt not only won a division championship (the first in twenty years) but he took Georgia's Bulldogs to a ranking of third in the nation. More remarkable than the team's progress was how he did it. Richt's focus wasn't and isn't on championships. It's on character.

A DIFFERENT KIND OF EDUCATION

"If you have good character, you're a diligent worker and you do what your coaches ask you to do," says Richt. "All of our players are talented, but the ones who don't have extra baggage of being in trouble academically, socially, or something else seem to rise to the top."

To focus on building the character in his athletes, Richt has introduced something into the football program at Georgia that's quite unusual. It's a fifteen-minute class several times a week called "Men of Character Between the Hedges." (The team's stadium is surrounded by hedges—thus the name.) The curriculum was brought to Georgia by Bobby Lankford, a former pro scout, who sometimes works with the players as a kind of character coach. Last season, the program was required of all freshmen. Eventually, all football players will take it. In fact, the course on character is so important that Georgia athletic director Vince Dooley would like to see an endowment created so that all Georgia athletes could be enrolled in it—someday maybe even for credit toward graduation.

Richt has gained the respect of his players not only through his coaching, but because of his own good character. That became evident to everyone following a game against Auburn his first year at Georgia. When he made a bad call in the remaining seconds of the game, his team lost. Richt didn't make excuses or place the blame on others. He apologized to the team for his mistake. Quarterback David Greene commented, "As a player you have respect for somebody who can come in and say he felt like he made a mistake. It's tough for anybody to admit a mistake, much less a football coach."[1]

Richt sees his role as that of improving others' lives, not just filling up the university's trophy case. That's something he seems to have a knack for. One sportswriter commented, "It's tough to find someone who has crossed Richt's path in the last 15 years who doesn't feel their way has been brightened by the convergence."[2]

In the future, when his players make mistakes—as they almost certainly will—his decisions will be based on character.

"Years from now," explains Richt, "if all these players are better men because they went to Georgia, I'd be thrilled. If a guy comes back and says he is a better man or better husband or father, or better citizen because of going through our program, that would mean more to me than a National Championship or high public opinion."

CHARACTER COUNTS

Recently I had the opportunity to meet Mark Richt and spend some time with him. I found him to be a man of strong character. He says his life turned around when he stopped focusing on himself. He brings consistent excellence to everything he does, but his focus is on helping people. Truly, he lives by the Golden Rule.

Only a person of character can impact others as Richt does. Character is the key to living a life of integrity and ethical excellence.

- **Character Is More Than Talk:** Many people talk about doing the right thing, but action is the true measure of character. Dennis Kozlowski, the CEO of Tyco, often touted the frugal way he conducted business and talked about the spartan offices the company maintained. However, anyone who watched his actions closely could have seen that his talk and walk didn't line up.
- **Talent Is a Gift—Character Is a Choice:** There are a lot of things in life a person doesn't get to choose, such as where you're born, who your parents are, and how tall you are. But there are some critical things every person does choose. We choose our faith, our attitude, and our character.
- **Character Brings Lasting Success with People:** Trust is essential when working with people. Character engenders trust. The people surrounding Mark Richt—his fellow coaches, players, family, and friends—know they can depend on him.
- **People Cannot Rise Above the Limitations of Their Character:** There are really only three kinds of people. Those who don't succeed, those who achieve success temporarily, and those who become and remain successful. Having character is the only way to sustain success. No matter how talented or rich or attractive people are, they will not be able to outrun their character.

THERE ARE REALLY ONLY THREE KINDS OF PEOPLE.
THOSE WHO DON'T SUCCEED, THOSE WHO ACHIEVE
SUCCESS TEMPORARILY, AND THOSE WHO BECOME
AND REMAIN SUCCESSFUL. CHARACTER IS THE
ONLY WAY TO SUSTAIN SUCCESS.

If you desire to live a life of character that exhibits ethical excellence, then follow these guidelines. They will help you to weave the Golden Rule into the fabric of your life:

1. Adopt the Golden Rule as the Integrity Guideline for Your Life

Swiss philosopher Henri Frederic Amiel stated, "He who floats with the current, who does not guide himself according to higher principles, who has no ideal, no convictions— such a man is a mere article of the world's furniture—a thing moved, instead of a living and moving being—an echo, not a voice." No one wants to be an echo, to live a shadow of a life. Yet that is often the fate of people without convictions. If you desire for your life to have meaning, then you must choose *some* principle to live by.

I've already made a case for the Golden Rule. *As I've said, asking the question "How would I like to be treated in this situation?" is an effective integrity guideline for* any *situation.* It works in the boardroom, on the ball field, in the classroom, and in the living room. It works with employees, employers, family, and peers. It works whether you're managing a paper route or a Fortune 500 company. As Henry Ford observed, "We have always found that if our principles were right, the area over which they were applied did not matter. Size is only a matter of the multiplication table."

If you believe the Golden Rule is right and it works, then you need to adopt it as the integrity guideline for your life. Every day, whenever the issue of ethical behavior confronts you, ask this question: "How would I like to be treated in this situation?" Then take the advice of nineteenth-century novelist George Eliot, who said, "Keep true, never be ashamed of doing right, decide on what you think is right and stick to it."

EVERY DAY, WHENEVER THE ISSUE OF ETHICAL BEHAVIOR CONFRONTS YOU, ASK THIS QUESTION: "HOW WOULD I LIKE TO BE TREATED IN THIS SITUATION?"

---

2. Make Your Decisions Based on This Integrity Guideline

Most people make only a few key decisions in life and then manage those decisions on a day-to-day basis. Once you decide to make the Golden Rule the integrity guideline for your life, you may have to rethink some of those decisions. How will the Golden Rule change your goals? Will you interact differently with your family? Will you need to change the way you approach your career? (Some people feel compelled to change jobs because their working environment is adverse to Golden Rule living.) Confucius asserted, "To know what is right and not do it is the worst cowardice." The bigger the decision, the more courage it may require.

Doing what's right when it hurts is no small thing. But the rewards are great. Horace Mann, former president of Antioch College, observed, "In vain do they talk of happiness who never subdued an impulse in obedience to a principle. He who never sacrificed a present to a future good, or a personal to a general one, can speak of happiness only as the blind speak of color."

As you apply the Golden Rule to your life and make decisions according to it, remember this:

- **Decisions, Not Conditions, Determine Your Ethics:** People of poor character tend to blame their choices on circumstances. Ethical people make good choices regardless of circumstances. If they make enough good choices, they begin to *create* better conditions for themselves.
- **Wrong Decisions Leave Scars:** Every time people make wrong decisions, there is an impact, even if they don't immediately notice it. My wife, Margaret, says that her grandmother used to tell her about a father who was trying to teach his son the consequences of bad decisions. Each time the boy made a poor decision, his father asked him to hammer a nail into a post. Each day that he made good choices, he was asked to remove a nail. In time, after much hammering and much pulling of nails, there came a day when the wood was nail-free. That's when the boy noticed that the post was covered with holes.

- **The More People Involved, the Greater the Pressure for Conformity:** Ethical decisions made in private have their own pressure, because one may be tempted to believe that a private indiscretion will never become public knowledge. Public decisions involving other people carry a different kind of pressure—that of conformity. No matter how much pressure there is, you can't allow others to force you into making unethical decisions.

- **Inaction Is Also a Decision:** Some people's reaction to ethical decision making is to avoid taking action. However, it's important to remember that inaction is also a decision. But for every Cynthia Cooper, who stepped forward and told WorldCom's board about the company's shady accounting practices, there are thousands of people who choose every day not to act when they see their employers cut corners or compromise ethics—and who ultimately will live with the consequences.

To live an ethical life, you must hold to your principles as you make tough decisions. Edward R. Lyman stated, "Principle—particularly moral principle—can never be a weather vane, spinning around this way and that with the shifting winds of expediency. Moral principle is a compass forever fixed and forever true—and that is as important in business as it is in the classroom."

3. Manage Your Decisions Based on This Integrity Guideline

Carole Black, the president and CEO of Lifetime Entertainment Services, the company that owns Lifetime Television, had to manage a tough decision in the spring of 2002. The company had made a commitment to a campaign called Stop Violence Against Women. All of the company's original programming was dedicated to supporting it. Going into February ratings sweeps, however, Black was convinced that Lifetime's ratings would suffer for it. She had to decide whether to change the network's programming or maintain the organization's commitment. She didn't falter.

"I warned top management that we were going to make this commitment," she recalls, "and that we'd probably get hurt in the ratings." To her surprise, Lifetime had their best February ever. "It's just like my grandmother taught me," says Black. "If you do the right thing, you'll be rewarded."[3]

When it comes to ethics, sometimes it's easy to make the big decisions. Most people don't have a tough time deciding *not* to commit murder. Few people are tempted to steal a car or break into someone's house. However, the little things can be harder to manage. There's an old saying, "God is in the details." You could also say ethics is in the details.

When I was just beginning to work on this book, I talked to my friend Ken Blanchard. He wrote a book with Norman Vincent Peale called *The Power of Ethical Management,* in which they ask three core questions for ethical decision making: Is it legal? Is it balanced? How will it make me feel about myself? I have a lot of respect for Ken. He told me a story that illustrates how critical it is to manage your decisions based on the Golden Rule:

One day an employee in Ken's company said to him, "I have a problem with your airfare."

"What's that?" he responded.

"You spoke for a client in Chicago last month, but you had already been flown there because of another commitment. When they signed the contract, they agreed to pay for a round-trip ticket. How am I to charge this client?"

What would you do in that situation? Would you ask for the entire fare since the client agreed to pay it? Or would you bill them only for the charge incurred? Ken chose to treat the clients as he would have liked to be treated in the same situation. He billed each client for half.

To be accounted trustworthy, a person must be predictable. When you manage your life and all the little decisions by one guideline—the Golden Rule—you create an ethical predictability in your life. People will have confidence in you, knowing that you consistently do the right thing.

WHEN YOU MANAGE YOUR LIFE AND ALL THE LITTLE DECISIONS BY ONE GUIDELINE—THE GOLDEN RULE—YOU CREATE AN ETHICAL PREDICTABILITY IN YOUR LIFE.

---

4. Ask Others to Hold You Accountable for Your Actions

Has someone ever stood looking over your shoulder as you worked on a project or task? If so, chances are you didn't like it. Most people don't. And they like it even less when some-one checks up on them to make sure they're being honest and responsible. Yet, that is what I'm suggesting you invite peo-ple to do if you want to live by the Golden Rule—because nothing helps to keep a person honest like accountability.

It's ironic. We don't like to be reminded of our shortcom-ings, and we don't like our shortcomings exposed to others either. But if we want to grow, we need to face the pain of exposing our actions to others. Integrity is the foundation of a person's life, and accountability is the cornerstone. It gives teeth to our pledge to live by high ethical standards.

In the U.S. Navy, officers are held accountable by their superiors. But former navy captain Mike Abrashoff, author of *It's Your Ship,* says that he held himself to a standard beyond even that required of him in the service. During his career, he continually subjected himself to the *Washington Post* test. He said that he wouldn't do anything he would not be proud to read about in the newspaper the next day. What a wonderful idea!

TRADING ON THE GOLDEN RULE

When you read about the lives of great men and women, you can tell when one of them lived a 24-karat-gold life. One of my favorites is the story of J. C. Penney, the founder of the department stores that bear his name. The son of a farmer, Penney grew up in Missouri. His father began forg-ing Penney's character early, teaching him industry, self-reliance, and the Golden Rule. For example, beginning when Penney was eight years old, he was required to earn enough money to buy his own clothes.

To make money, Penney worked and scraped together $2.50 to buy a young pig. Then he did chores for neighbors in order to gather slops for the animal and fattened it up. When he sold it during slaughtering season, he made a nice profit. Seeing the benefits of such an arrangement, he bought a dozen piglets the next season, and he gathered corn from the farm's rows after the huskers were finished harvesting. The pigs were growing nicely, and Penney expected to make a great profit in the fall. But then one day his father made him sell them because the neighbors were complaining about the smell. Penney commented, "It was the off season for pork . . . but my father lived by the Golden Rule in relation to his neighbors, and it was important to him for me to see that I should too."[4]

As Penney got older, he found that he had a knack for trading, and he continually worked at it. Meanwhile, his father encouraged him and made sure he was always scrupulously honest. He also helped his son get his first job in a dry goods store in Hamilton, Missouri. There J. C. Penney learned his trade. In time he moved on to other stores, always working hard and treating others as he wanted to be treated. At one store, when he discovered that the same socks were priced several different ways in order to take advantage of unwitting customers, he resigned. Eventually he got on with a store in which he was invited to become a partner. He was so good at his trade, the men offered him a partnership in additional stores they intended to open. And when the original owners wanted to leave the business in 1907, Penney bought them out.

Penney had a vision for a chain of stores all across the western United States. His method was to find honest, industrious men and teach them his method of business. And if they succeeded in managing their store well and turned around and trained another man to do the same, he would offer them partnership in a new store, just as it had been offered to him. "I think, if we pick the right kind of men and train them the right way, they will all catch the spirit of partnership idea," he told the first manager he invited to become part owner of a store.[5]

And what were those original stores called? He named them for his philosophy of business. They were called the Golden Rule stores. "Hence," explained Penney, "in setting up a business under the name and meaning of the Golden Rule, I was publicly binding myself, in my business relations, to a principle which had been a real and intimate part of my family upbringing. To me the sign on the store was much more than a trade name."[6]

Though Penney later changed the names on the stores when his organization incorporated during expansion, he never stopped living—and working—by the Golden Rule, putting partnership ahead of profits. He stated his philosophy succinctly: "Money is properly the byproduct of building men as partners."[7]

Penney continued to work and create partners for many years. He finally turned the business over to one of the people he'd made a partner—a man who'd worked for him in one of the first stores. Penney lived a 24-karat-gold life, treating others with respect, giving them value in business, and providing the best merchandise he could procure. He lived to be ninety-five years old.

There's an old saying that when you get squeezed, whatever is in you will come out. I believe that is true. But I also know that a person cannot develop a 24-karat-gold life overnight. Penney was fortunate. His parents trained him in the Golden Rule from infancy, and he embraced it all his life. If you've had that kind of upbringing, thank your parents. If you haven't, it's still not too late to change. Thomas Addington and Stephen Graves, editors of *Life@Work* magazine, observe, "We cannot grow character through a crash-course weekend seminar when one day we suddenly realize we need some. It's impossible. We can't become an astronaut, or a world-class fly fisherman, or an expert brick mason in a microwave weekend of learning."[8] Begin today by adopting the Golden Rule as your integrity guideline and then manage your decisions by it. And you, too, will be able to live a 24-karat-gold life.

5

Five Factors That Can "Tarnish" the Golden Rule

IN CHAPTER 4 I TOLD YOU ABOUT MARK RICHT AND HOW HIS focus on character building has paid off in the Georgia Bulldogs' success and a high national ranking. But sometimes ethical decisions don't have that kind of happy ending. That was the case for Mike Slaughter, head football coach of Marquette Catholic High School in Alton, Illinois.

During the 2002 season, Slaughter had what he called a "once in a lifetime team." Their record was 10-0, and they were on track to earn the school's first state championship. Slaughter was living out every coach's dream. But then one night, sixteen of his players—all starters—were arrested for underage drinking at a party. And the group included Slaughter's own son. The coach had always told his players that if they got in trouble with alcohol, tobacco, or drugs, he would suspend them from the team. So he had a decision to make.

He suspended the players. "It boils down to accountability," explained Slaughter. "They broke the rules." And he told his son, whom he picked up from the sheriff's office, "Son, all I can tell you is you messed up. I'll always love you, but you need to learn from this."

The suspended players did learn, and when the big game came, they suited up and sat on the bench to encourage their teammates. And did the second- and third-string players step up and win the big game for their ethical coach and go on to capture the state championship? No. Marquette lost 63–0. But Slaughter has no regrets about his decision. In years past, he had received calls telling him someone he knew had been killed while driving drunk. He knows he made the right decision and says, "It's strange that we get this much publicity for doing what we consider the right thing."[1]

UNDERMINING THE GOLDEN RULE

Doing the right thing does get a lot of attention these days. Why is that? Because it's news when someone practices the Golden Rule, experiences negative consequences for it, and is content that he did the right thing.

Let's face it, there are lots of things that entice people to cross an ethical line. As I've worked with people and led organizations for more than thirty-five years, I have unfortunately seen many people compromise their standards. And I can tell you that having worked with people in just about every socioeconomic group in more than a dozen countries around the world, I believe it usually boils down to five things. These are the five factors that most often come into play when someone compromises his ethics:

1. Pressure

Many of the ethical violations that keep emerging in corporate America today are due to executives' "cooking the books." They do it to make their organizations appear more successful than they are. That was apparently the case at Enron. Cynthia Harkness, an Enron lawyer, recounted that CFO Andrew Fastow introduced her to the concept of monetization in which future revenue is booked immediately. She told him, "Andy, it seems to me that if you do a 10-year deal, and suck all the earnings out in one year, you will then have to keep the profit coming through years 4, 5, 6, and all the way to 10, by doing more of these deals. . . . How are you going to do that if the market changes? Book more deals?"

"Yes," she says he responded, "you have to keep doing more of these deals each year."[2] And with each deal, the pressure to book more deals would continue to build. That had to end somewhere—and it did: with Enron's implosion.

According to Linda Treviño, professor of organizational behavior at Penn State's Smeal College of Business Administration, "Ethical breaches are often the result of the corporate culture or pressure from management, pressure that can emerge when a company finds itself unable to live up to financial forecasts or expectations and tries to bend the rules to achieve them."[3]

In our fast-paced culture, I think just about everyone feels some kind of pressure. And with pressure comes the temptation to cut corners or bend the truth. Corporate executives feel pressure to increase stock value. Salespeople feel pressure to make more sales. Students feel pressure to get higher grades. No one escapes pressure. So the question is: How are you going to deal with it?

As you face pressure, beware of how you might be tempted to compromise your values, and ask yourself some tough questions:

- **Am I Going to Make Rash Emotional Decisions?** Pressure creates tension, and tension can make for some emotional moments. Some people have a hard time in such situations, and they make poor decisions that impact themselves or others. How can I guard against that?
- **Am I Going to Compromise the Truth?** Some people find it almost impossible to admit making a mistake. Am I willing to stick with the truth even when I don't like it?
- **Am I Going to Take Shortcuts?** Someone once said that the longest distance between two points is a shortcut. While that may be true, pressure tempts us to consider shortcuts when we otherwise wouldn't. Am I willing to fight to do what's right?
- **Am I Going to Keep My Commitments?** Molière said, "Men are alike in their promises. It is only in their deeds that they differ." Am I going to keep my word and follow through, even when it hurts?
- **Am I Going to Bow to Others' Opinions?** Some people are especially susceptible to the opinions of others. That was true of me the first five years of my career. Will I do what I know is right, even when it's unpopular?
- **Am I Going to Make Promises I Can't Keep?** Samuel Johnson said, "We ought not to raise expectations which

"MEN ARE ALIKE IN THEIR PROMISES. IT IS ONLY IN THEIR
DEEDS THAT THEY DIFFER."—MOLIÈRE

it is not in our power to satisfy. It is more pleasing to see
smoke brightening into flame, than flame sinking into
smoke." How am I going to keep my promises from
going up in smoke?

In order for me to make good decisions under pressure, I
need reminders of what's at stake. First, I'm accountable to
God. Second, I'm accountable to my family. And I keep
reminders of that around me all the time. In my office I have
pictures of Margaret along with my children and grandchildren so I'll never forget that people are depending on me to
do right. One of my definitions of success is for those closest to me to love and respect me the most.

Reminders are valuable, but they are not enough. I also
need systems to keep me on track. For example, if I must
make a decision under pressure, I will take the time to write
out the problem and solution so I won't act rashly. I write
down promises I make so I cannot easily forget them. I also
ask my assistant, Linda Eggers, to follow up with me on
decisions and promises so they don't slip through the
cracks. I suggest that you do similar kinds of things. Do
whatever you must to hold up under pressure.

2. *Pleasure*

In *The Road Less Traveled,* psychiatrist M. Scott Peck tells a story about how he received a new bicycle when he was nine years old. One of the things he discovered was the thrill of riding his bike fast down a hill. But he soon learned that unchecked thrill-seeking can lead to pain. On one occasion, as he zoomed down the hill he decided that he would try to take the curve at the bottom of the incline without slowing down. He experienced a terrible crash. He says, "I had been unwilling to suffer the pain of giving up my ecstatic speed in the interest of maintaining my balance around the corner."[4]

Peck's childhood experience isn't much different from how many adults live their entire lives. Let's face it, we live in a hedonistic society. For decades, people in America were encouraged by the words "If it feels good, do it." But that attitude has left us with a terrible legacy: runaway debt and bankruptcy, divorce, and drug addiction. The desire for pleasure can be a terrible master. The fact is that the pleasures most of us pursue are short-lived and leave us unfulfilled. The things that tempt us rarely deliver on what they promise. Poet Robert Browning Hamilton gave insight into that truth when he wrote these words:

> I walked a mile with Pleasure,
>   She chattered all the way,
> But she left me none the wiser,
>   For all she had to say.
> I walked a mile with Sorrow,
>   And ne'er a word said she;

But, oh, the things I learned from her
When Sorrow walked with me![5]

If we allow it to, the desire for pleasure (or comfort) will talk us into doing things we will regret afterward.

What is the answer to the lure of pleasure? The first is to run from temptation. In *Following the Equator* Mark Twain observed, "There are several good precautions against temptation, but the surest is cowardice." If you know you are especially susceptible to a pleasure that would tempt you to cross an ethical line, put yourself out of harm's way. When you see it coming, cross to the other side of the street. The best way to avoid temptation is to prevent it.

The second key is to develop discipline. In *Reasons to Be Glad,* author Richard Foster writes,

The disciplined person is the person who can do what needs to be done when it needs to be done. The disciplined person is the person who can live in the appropriateness of the hour. The extreme ascetic and the glutton have exactly the same problem: they cannot live appropriately; they cannot do what needs to be done when it needs to be done. The disciplined person is the free person.[6]

"THE DISCIPLINED PERSON IS THE PERSON WHO CAN DO WHAT NEEDS TO BE DONE WHEN IT NEEDS TO BE DONE."—RICHARD FOSTER

It's ironic, but to gain freedom, you need to contain your emotions with discipline. That takes character. One of the best ways to develop discipline is to delay gratification.

Our generation does not do that well. We are microwave people; we want everything now. My parents' generation, who survived the Great Depression and fought World War II, seems more disciplined. David Callahan, in *Kindred Spirits: Harvard Business School's Extraordinary Class of 1949,* examined one postwar class of graduates that was comprised of 91 percent veterans. He compared those graduates, who went on to lead many major corporations, such as Johnson & Johnson and Capital Cities/ABC, with average chief executives today. "Now," writes Callahan, "there's very little sense of sacrifice, of having to defer gratification. It's more about getting something for themselves."[7]

Business leaders who have lost their hearts to pleasure and possessions regrettably make themselves untrustworthy to their followers. Anyone who loves pleasure more than truth is headed for trouble—and will take others with him.

3. Power

Many of the recent scandals in American business have developed because executives abused the power of their positions. They began to think that the assets of the publicly traded companies they led could be treated as their personal property. Unfortunately, for many people, having power is like drinking salt water. The more you drink, the thirstier you get. The founding fathers of our country recognized this and created a government with three branches so there would be checks and balances on power. For, as U.S. President John Adams said, "No man is wise enough or good enough to be trusted with unlimited power."

Harriet Rubin, the author of two books on power, calls self-centered bosses who thrive on power "executive narcissists." She describes them in this way: "They do the boozing, and you get the headache.... They never say thank you, and they use people like Kleenex."[8] Leadership expert and psychoanalyst Abraham Zaleznik says that many executives develop a sense of entitlement. Such an executive "comes to believe that he and the institution are one. So . . . that he can take what he wants when he wants it."[9]

Bruce Horovitz of *USA Today* has a humorous take on this kind of behavior. He calls what's happening in corporate America the *"Yertle the Turtle* syndrome."[10] In the book of that title by Dr. Seuss, Yertle, the king turtle who is master of all he can see, enlarges his kingdom by ordering all his subjects to stack themselves into a tower with him at the top. But the whole thing comes crashing down in the end.

People who are especially susceptible to power issues typically experience a cycle that follows this pattern:

- **The Reception of Power:** Power itself is neutral, like money. It's a tool that can be used for good or ill. But it can be dangerous, especially for people who achieve success quickly and easily and receive power before they are ready for it.

- **The Abuse of Power:** One of the dangers of power is that those who are entrusted with it begin to make its preservation their primary concern. They don't understand that the power they have been given—whether it's in business, government, ministry, or relationships—has been bestowed on them for the purpose of service. Those who want most to keep their power at all costs are most likely to compromise standard ethical behavior to keep it.
- **The Loss of Power:** Inevitably, anyone who abuses power loses power. Abusive CEOs, like dictators, are living on borrowed time.

Abusers of power see things in much the way Robert Greene, author of *The 48 Laws of Power,* sees them. He recommends a course of action that runs a different direction from the Golden Rule. He writes,

Keep people off-balance and in the dark by never revealing the purpose behind your actions. If they have no clue what you are up to, they cannot prepare a defense. Guide them far enough down the wrong path, envelop them in smoke, and by the time they realize your intentions, it will be too late. . . . Reputation is the cornerstone of power. Through reputation alone you can intimidate and win; once it slips, however, you are vulnerable, and will be attacked on all sides. Make your reputation unassailable.[11]

A person's image, which Greene describes as "reputation," is like a shadow, but character is the actual substance of the person. To achieve long-term success and live an ethical life, don't worry about creating a good image. You would be better off working to make your *character* unassailable.

Power is like a mighty river. As long as it keeps its course, it is a useful thing of beauty. But when it floods its banks, it brings great destruction. How does one keep power in its banks? Take the advice of U.S. President Harry Truman. He recommended, "If a man can accept a situation in a place of power with the thought that it's only temporary, he comes out all right. But when he thinks he is the *cause* of the power, that can be his ruination." Anyone who realizes that he's guarding his power too much had better start examining himself for breaches of ethics. Power can be terribly seductive.

"IF A MAN CAN ACCEPT A SITUATION IN A PLACE OF POWER WITH THE THOUGHT THAT IT'S ONLY TEMPORARY, HE COMES OUT ALL RIGHT. BUT WHEN HE THINKS HE IS THE CAUSE OF THE POWER, THAT CAN BE HIS RUINATION."

—HARRY TRUMAN

---

4. Pride

You may not automatically think of pride as a potential pitfall that can undermine ethics and work against the practice of the Golden Rule. After all, aren't people exhorted to take pride in their work? Don't we reward our children's good behavior by telling them how proud we are of them? Aren't students encouraged to develop pride in their school?

Having a sense of worth because of who you are is a good thing. So is having confidence in what you can do. However, having an exaggerated sense of self-worth can be highly destructive. Wisdom literature is filled with warnings concerning pride and its negative impact. Take a look at these statements about pride—taken from just the book of Proverbs:

"PRIDE IS AT THE BOTTOM OF ALL GREAT MISTAKES."
—JOHN RUSKIN

- Pride goes before destruction.[12]
- When pride comes, then comes disgrace.[13]
- Pride only breeds quarrels.[14]
- A man's pride brings him low.[15]

Nineteenth-century writer and art critic John Ruskin asserted, "Pride is at the bottom of all great mistakes." What is it about pride that is so negative? Professor, writer, and Christian apologist C. S. Lewis offered a perspective on pride with great insight. He believed that pride leads to every other vice. He remarked,

Does this seem to you exaggerated? If so, think it over. I pointed out a moment ago that the more pride one had, the more one disliked pride in others. In fact, if you want to find out how proud you are the easiest way is to ask yourself, "How much do I dislike it when other people snub me, or refuse to take any notice of me? . . ." The point is that each person's pride is in competition with everyone else's pride. It is because I wanted to be the big noise at the party that I am so annoyed at someone else being the big noise. . . . Now what you want to get clear is that Pride is essentially competitive, is competitive by its very nature, while the other vices are competitive only, so to speak, by accident.

Pride gets no pleasure out of having something, only out of having more of it than the next man. We say that people are proud of being richer, or cleverer, or better looking than others. If everyone else became equally rich, or clever, or good looking there would be nothing to be proud about. It is the comparison that makes you proud: the pleasure of being above the rest.[16]

How can people treat others the way they want to be treated if their preoccupation is to *beat* them? They can't. In fact, if your goal is to be richer, smarter, or better looking than everyone else, your focus is entirely on yourself and your own interests.

Several years ago, *Time* magazine noted a decline in ethics in American business, politics, law, and medicine, and they attributed the slide to pride. In a "protective obsession with self and image" a *Time* writer concluded, members of these professions tended to "sweep ethics complaints under the rug."[17]

Pride is not an easy thing to conquer. Benjamin Franklin observed that "there is perhaps not one of our natural passions so hard to subdue as pride. Beat it down, stifle it, mortify it as much as one pleases, it is still alive. Even if I could conceive that I had completely overcome it, I should probably be proud of my humility." Yet we *should* work to overcome pride. Not only does it have the potential to undermine our ethics, it can also interfere with our performance. Peggy Noonan quotes a nineteenth-century German diplomat who said that while it may be tough to trick an honest man, it's easy to fool someone who thinks himself clever.[18] Pride can blind you—to your own faults, to other people's needs, and to ethical pitfalls that lie in your path.

5. Priorities

Jim Collins, the author of *Built to Last* and *Good to Great,* has done extensive research into what makes companies highly successful. When he recently was asked what his research indicated about the importance of ethics in building a successful company, Collins replied, "Our research points to one essential element in any successful company.

"THINGS THAT MATTER MOST MUST NEVER BE AT THE MERCY OF THINGS THAT MATTER LEAST."—GOETHE

Those that are the best have built a set of core values and lived by them."[19]

The same is true for individuals. Any time a person doesn't know what his priorities are, he can find himself in trouble because he is liable to make poor decisions. German poet and novelist Johann Wolfgang von Goethe advised, "Things that matter most must never be at the mercy of things that matter least."

I must admit, this has been an area of weakness for me at times. When I took my first job as a pastor, my priorities were out of whack. Back then I wanted most to be liked by people. That sometimes prompted me to make poor decisions. Once when my people pleasing led me to fail in a major responsibility, I experienced a crisis that caused me to come to grips with my priorities. It was during that time I determined God would be first in my life, my family would be second, and my work would be a distant third. That doesn't mean the fight is over. Every day I still have to manage my decisions based on those priorities. It's one thing to define your values. It's another to live them out every day.

What are your priorities? In fifty or a hundred years what are you doing now that will still be important? The house you live in, the car you drive, the vacation you took, and the bonus you made won't mean much. What really matters? If you haven't defined your values, I encourage you to do so. Then work hard to keep the unimportant from becoming important, and the important from becoming unimportant.

KEEPING AWAY THE TARNISH

You may have noticed that greed didn't make the list of factors that can "tarnish" the Golden Rule. That might have come as a surprise, especially since the press have talked so much about it recently with all the corporate scandals. But I believe that, most of the time, it's not the money itself that draws people across the line ethically. It's what they can get with it. They want the power that money can bring, whether it's power over people or over circumstances. Or they want the pleasure that can be bought. Or they take pride in the prestige of possessions. If you find someone who will compromise integrity for money, I believe you will discover that it is motivated by one of the five factors I've mentioned.

Everyone is susceptible to some kind of temptation to compromise values. But there is a greater satisfaction that comes from *not* crossing the line. Sometimes you have to wait for it, but it always comes. I believe that someday, maybe twenty years from now, one of Coach Mike Slaughter's players will come to him and tell him how being suspended from his high school football team changed his life and made him a better person. On that day, Slaughter will be rewarded by something more valuable than a mere state championship.

6

Seizing Your Golden Opportunity

I THINK JUST ABOUT EVERYBODY IS LOOKING FOR A GOLDEN opportunity. Businesspeople in particular possess a keen eye for such things. Recently I asked my research assistant, Kathie Wheat, to search the Web for a "golden opportunity." She reported that in less than one-fourth of a second, the search engine Google returned 1,310,000 hits on that phrase. You name it, and there was an offer for it, claiming to be a golden opportunity. You could buy fried chicken restaurant franchises or bride's jewelry. You could sign up for yoga classes, get tips on hot stocks, or engage in multi-family recycling of solid waste. There was even an offer to develop recombinant proteins in chicken eggs—whatever that means!

How do you find a true golden opportunity among all the offers that are really made of lead? You don't look outside yourself. Most people think their greatest opportunities come from a job, an investment, or a market niche. But the truth is that the greatest opportunity you have is to

YOU CAN'T CAPITALIZE ON AN OPPORTUNITY YOU
RECEIVE ON THE OUTSIDE UNTIL YOU'VE DONE THE
GROUNDWORK ON THE INSIDE.

change who *you* are. It's like offering a position on the Olympics team to someone who hasn't trained for their event. The good news is that he has been granted a shot at winning. The bad news is that he's not ready for it.

ONE THING LEADS TO ANOTHER

I suspect that was the problem for some of the CEOs who ruined their careers and destroyed their companies in recent years. They hadn't done the ethical groundwork on the inside before attaining power. Their weak character prompted them to make bad decisions, and with each poor choice, they got into deeper trouble. Character problems tend to snowball. C. S. Lewis gave insight into the process using a military metaphor. He explained,

> Good and evil both increase at compound interest. That is why the little decisions you and I make every day are of such infinite importance. The smallest good act today is the capture of a strategic point from which, a few months later, you may be able to go on to victories you never dreamed of. An apparently trivial indulgence in lust or in anger today is the loss of a ridge or railway line or bridgehead from which the enemy may launch an attack otherwise impossible.[1]

If you want to be able to pursue golden opportunities, then pursue the development of strong character first. That

---

A PERSON OF RESPONSIBILITY CAN TRUST HIMSELF TO CHOOSE
THE RIGHT THING OVER THE EASY THING.

---

will position you well to face any ethical challenges that may lie ahead and to make the most of your chances when your time comes. Here's how I suggest you proceed:

1. Take Responsibility for Your Actions

U.S. President Woodrow Wilson observed, "Responsibility is proportionate to opportunity." Why is that? Because a person of responsibility can trust himself to choose the right thing over the easy thing. He takes to heart the words of historian Will Durant, who said, "Never mind your happiness; do your duty."

I once heard someone say that frustration is "having no one to blame but yourself." But rarely do people who play the blame game get many golden opportunities. And even the few opportunities they do get slip through their fingers. When that happens, you hear why it's not their fault. Their excuses fall into three categories:

- The Hang-ups—who blame life's circumstances,
- The Bang-ups—who blame past personal problems and hurts, and
- The Gang-ups—who blame other people for hindering them.

If you desire to be trusted by others and you want to achieve much, you must take responsibility for your actions. Winston Churchill was right when he called responsibility "the price of greatness." It's also the groundwork for opportunity.

2. Develop Personal Discipline

I recently saw the results of a survey that said 82 percent of corporate executives admit to cheating at golf, and 72 percent believe actions in business and golf parallel each other.[2] Why is it that even when people see a parallel between games and life, they still choose to cut corners? I believe the answer is that they lack discipline. People who fail to develop personal discipline are often tempted to cheat to keep up. In the words of H. Jackson Brown, "Talent without discipline is like an octopus on roller skates. There's plenty of movement, but you never know if it's going to be forward, backwards, or sideways."

Nineteenth-century clergyman and Oxford University professor H. P. Liddon said, "What we do on some great occasion will probably depend on what we already are; and what we are will be the result of previous years of self-discipline." People

---

"WHAT WE DO ON SOME GREAT OCCASION WILL PROBABLY DEPEND ON WHAT WE ALREADY ARE; AND WHAT WE ARE WILL BE THE RESULT OF PREVIOUS YEARS OF SELF-DISCIPLINE."

—H. P. LIDDON

---

who desire to improve their character and their chances of success must discipline themselves when it comes to. . . .

- **Time:** Since you can't control how much time you have, you must control how you use it.
- **Energy:** You should always strive to use your strength on your strengths.
- **Goals:** You can't do everything, so you must discipline yourself to do the important things.
- **Moods:** If you do not master your emotions, they will master you.

Successful people who work well with others and who relish challenges as well as opportunities don't see discipline as negative or restrictive. They welcome it. Vince Lombardi, legendary coach of the NFL Green Bay Packers, asserted, "I've never known a man worth his salt who in the long run, deep down in his heart, didn't appreciate the grind, the discipline."

3. Know Your Weaknesses

One evening at Sagamore Hill, President Theodore Roosevelt's home in New York, naturalist William Beebe walked outside with his host. Roosevelt searched the star-filled night sky and, finding a small glow below the corner of the constellation Pegasus, he said, "This is the spiral galaxy Andromeda. It is as large as our Milky Way. It consists of one hundred billion suns. It is one of a hundred billion galaxies." Then Roosevelt looked at Beebe and said, "Now, I think we are small enough! Let's go to bed."[3]

Theodore Roosevelt was very good at keeping things in perspective. Part of that came from knowing himself and his weaknesses. As I explained in *The 21 Irrefutable Laws of Leadership,* Roosevelt was weak, sickly, asthmatic, and underweight as a child. Recognizing this, he dedicated himself to strengthening his body. He went on to work as a cowboy, hunt wild game, fight in battles as a cavalry officer, and box. He changed from being a puny boy to being our most vigorous president.

To be forewarned is to be forearmed. People who know their weakness are rarely taken by surprise, nor do they allow others to exploit their areas of weakness. In contrast, people who deceive themselves or who pretend to be strong where they're not set themselves up for failure.

4. Align Your Priorities with Your Values

Integrity can be described as making your beliefs and your actions line up. When individuals say they believe one thing and then deliberately do something else, it's obvious that they lack integrity. But how about someone who doesn't realize that his actions contradict his beliefs? Even though it's not deliberate, that person still has an integrity problem.

INTEGRITY CAN BE DESCRIBED AS MAKING YOUR BELIEFS AND YOUR ACTIONS LINE UP.

The most basic definition of *integrity* includes the idea that something or someone is whole and complete. If you're asserting one thing but doing another, you're divided. And as President Abraham Lincoln asserted, a house divided against itself cannot stand. The solution is simple, though not necessarily easy. Define your values; then align your priorities.

5. Admit Wrongdoing Quickly and Ask Forgiveness

One thing that has characterized nearly all the recent high-profile business breakdowns has been some kind of cover-up. Executives at Enron, Tyco, and WorldCom all tried to hide any wrongdoing. Of course, that attitude isn't pervasive just in business. People of poor character in every profession are quicker to cover up than they are to confess wrongdoing.

Look at the case of Robert Torricelli, a former U.S. senator from New Jersey. After accepting numerous gifts and more than $53,000 in illegal campaign contributions from a supporter, Torricelli maintained that he had done nothing wrong—even after the Senate Ethics Committee "severely admonished" him.[4] And when he later dropped out of the race for his seat in the Senate, his departure speech was self-righteous. At one point he defended his career, saying, "That's my life. . . . I'm proud of every day of it. And I wouldn't change a bit of it." But he later lamented, "When did we become such an unforgiving people? . . . When did we stop believing in and trusting in each other?"[5] People are more forgiving and trusting when individuals who make mistakes are truthful about them and ask for forgiveness.

Contrast the actions of Torricelli with those of Harry

Kraemer, CEO of medical supply manufacturer Baxter International. In 2001, when dialysis patients using his company's filters started dying, he recalled the products as a precaution, launched an internal investigation, and hired experts to search for possible flaws. And he quickly extended his condolences to the families of the affected patients. Ultimately, although Kraemer could have exercised damage control and tried to place the blame elsewhere, he instead pulled the product from the market, and shut down that division of the company, costing Baxter $189 million. And he reported the problem to rival manufacturers who might experience similar difficulties. He did it because it was the right thing. He also recommended to the board's compensation committee that his performance bonus be reduced by at least forty percent for 2001.

Kraemer has been described as being relentlessly authentic. "Harry lives his life the way most of us would like to live our lives," says Donald P. Jacobs, dean emeritus at the Kellogg School. "What Harry says he believes in, you can put it in the bank. The way he treats his coworkers is the way he'd like people to treat him."[6] Kraemer made the best of a terrible situation with integrity by acting according to the Golden Rule. Who could ask for more than that?

6. *Take Extra Care with Finances*

If you want to know something about the character of individuals, watch how they handle money. (Automaker Henry Ford remarked, "Money doesn't change men, it merely unmasks them. If a man is naturally selfish or arrogant or

> "MONEY DOESN'T CHANGE MEN, IT MERELY UNMASKS THEM.
> IF A MAN IS NATURALLY SELFISH OR ARROGANT OR GREEDY,
> THE MONEY BRINGS THAT OUT, THAT IS ALL."—HENRY FORD

greedy, the money brings that out, that is all.") Are people generous with others' money but tight with their own? Do they insist that every transaction clearly benefit them? Do they cut corners to gain more wealth? What place does money have in their lives?

People are often tripped up when they make accumulating wealth a higher priority than it should be. That was the mythical king Midas's problem. He put money first in his life, and it almost cost him everything. Stoic philosopher Zeno of Citium said, "The avaricious man is like the barren sandy ground in the desert which sucks in all the rain and dew with greediness, but yields no fruitful herbs or plants for the benefit of others."

I mentioned in Chapter 5 that money is nothing more than a tool. But it is a sharp tool, one that if handled poorly can do great harm. That's why we should always take extra care with finances. If we can maintain the right attitude about money, then it will always be a positive, helpful tool, not a destructive one. As P. T. Barnum observed, "Money is a terrible master but an excellent servant." To keep money from becoming a master, I recommend doing the following:

- **Earn Your Money:** People who earn what they have possess a greater respect for the possessions of others.

And they often try to get more bang for their buck if they have to earn it themselves.

- **Be Scrupulously Honest:** Bend over backward to make sure all your financial dealings are aboveboard, not only for the sake of others, but also for yourself. B. C. Forbes observed, "He is a wise man who seeks by every legitimate means to make all the money he can honestly, for money can do so many worthwhile things in this world, not merely for one's self but for others. But he is an unmitigated fool who imagines for a moment that it is more important to make the money than to make it honestly."

- **Be Generous:** It's been said that we make a living by what we get; we make a life by what we give. Giving not only helps others and frees us, it also puts money into perspective better than anything else we can do.

- **Use Credit Wisely and Sparingly:** King Solomon advised, "The rich rules over the poor, and the borrower becomes the lender's slave."[7] To maintain your freedom, refrain from incurring debt.

"THERE IS NO DIGNITY QUITE SO IMPRESSIVE AND NO INDEPENDENCE QUITE SO IMPORTANT AS LIVING WITHIN YOUR MEANS."—CALVIN COOLIDGE

President Calvin Coolidge said, "There is no dignity quite so impressive and no independence quite so important as living within your means." Learning to have the right attitude toward money and to handle it well (instead of being handled by it) paves the way for many other character victories in a person's life.

7. Put Your Family Ahead of Your Work

The list of titles and positions he has earned is impressive: U.S. congressman, ambassador to the United Nations, chief liaison officer in China, head of the CIA, vice president of the United States, and, finally, president of the United States. But when his life in public office ended, the elder George Bush said that he still possessed the three most important titles he had ever held: husband, father, and grandfather. That's a great perspective on family.

Unfortunately, many people in our culture seem willing to set their families aside because they think they must in order to get ahead in their careers. The divorce rate bears that out. So does the failure of noncustodial parents to follow through on their financial obligations. Each year, $20 to $30 *billion* in taxpayers' money goes to support children whose parents neglect them financially.[8]

But in the long run, making your family a priority doesn't hurt your career; it actually helps it. As NBA coach Pat Riley says, "Sustain a family for a long period of time and you can sustain success for a long period of time. First things first. If your life is in order, you can do whatever you want." Having a strong and stable family creates a launching pad for many other successes during a career and provides a contented landing place at the end of it.

8. *Place High Value on People*

When most people think of developing character, they focus on what they must become, which is good, since that is the majority of the process. But to make yourself ready to seize golden opportunities, you must do something more. You must value others enough to give them a part of yourself—your trust. That, after all, is really the essence of the Golden Rule.

In *Winning Management: Six Fail-Safe Strategies for Building High-Performance Organizations,* Wolf J. Rinke writes, "If you mistrust your employees, you'll be right 3 percent of the time. If you trust people until they give you a reason not to, you'll be right 97 percent of the time."[9] Those are pretty good odds.

"IF YOU MISTRUST YOUR EMPLOYEES, YOU'LL BE RIGHT 3 PERCENT OF THE TIME. IF YOU TRUST PEOPLE UNTIL THEY GIVE YOU A REASON NOT TO, YOU'LL BE RIGHT 97 PERCENT OF THE TIME."—WOLF J. RINKE

As I began working on this book, one of the people I talked to about the concept was Mike Abrashoff, author of *It's Your Ship: Management Techniques from the Best Damn Ship in the Navy.*[10] We got to know each other when he spoke at a conference my company hosted. Mike is the epitome of someone who was ready for his golden opportunity when it came and who achieved success by practicing the Golden Rule.

Before Mike took his first command, which was of the

USS *Benfold,* he had already been successful. He had graduated from the U.S. Naval Academy at Annapolis. He had excelled as an officer, attaining the rank of captain after sixteen years, and had worked as military assistant to Dr. William J. Perry when he was Secretary of Defense. But when Mike took command of the *Benfold,* he saw it as a rare opportunity to do something different, to use a Golden Rule approach to leadership. Mike says,

> The first sixteen years of my career, I went for the gold braid. I had success, but it wasn't unusual success. The last two I went for the Golden Rule. I took command of the ship and took command of my life. Before, I was working according to what I thought were the organization's expectations. But while working for Secretary of Defense Perry, I saw a departure from that kind of thinking. When I saw my predecessor leaving the ship, I thought about what my departure would be like.
>
> The navy is like a tree full of monkeys. If you're at the top of the tree, all you see when you look down is a bunch of smiling faces looking up to you. When you're at the bottom of the tree and you look up, you have a different kind of view![11]

Mike decided to put himself in the shoes of his sailors. He individually interviewed every sailor on his ship to find out what they valued, and then he made changes to add value to them, such as sending the ship's cooks to culinary school and offering college courses aboard ship. He asked his officers to treat the new arrivals as they would want their own children treated. And he empowered everyone—officer and enlisted person alike—to make decisions and work to make their ship the best in the navy, trusting them and encouraging them with the words: "It's your ship."

"Good began to happen when I began going for the Golden Rule," says Mike. "I put people instead of promotion first. And as a result, I was paid a thousand times over." That's what I call making the most of a golden opportunity.

7

How to Develop the "Midas Touch"

WHEN I WAS A KID, I LEARNED ABOUT GREEK MYTHOLOGY IN school. One of the stories that always stuck with me was that of King Midas. He was the king of ancient Phrygia. One day he gave assistance to an old friend of Dionysus, the god of revelry, and as a reward, Midas was granted one wish. He asked Dionysus to make everything he touched turn to gold. When his wish was granted, he touched a tree—and it turned to gold. He touched a horse—and it became solid gold. In a matter of minutes, he was becoming the richest man in the world.

His trouble started when he got hungry. He sat down at a banquet table, and the meat he reached for turned to solid gold as soon as he touched it. The same happened to the wine he tried to drink. But the worst thing happened when his daughter hugged him. She instantly became a golden statue. In the end, Midas begged Dionysus to take his golden power away from him. Dionysus sent Midas to the source of the river Pactolus, where he was to bathe in order to be restored to normal. He went, taking his daughter with him, and ultimately both were changed back to their previous state. Only after Midas lost his golden ability was he happy again.

REAL GOLD

Today, when someone is told that he has the "Midas touch," it's usually meant as a compliment. It's an indication he has a great knack for making money. But a single-minded fixation on wealth is just as damaging to a person today as it was during the time of the ancient Greeks. American publisher and businessman B. C. Forbes, who founded *Forbes* magazine, commented:

> Are your desires purely selfish? Do your tastes run to a grand home, automobiles, fine clothes, an abundance of amusements, and so forth? If so, look around you at people who have such things in superabundance. Are they any happier, do you think, than you are? Are they any better morally? Are they any stronger physically? Are they better liked by their friends than you are by your friends? . . . Carnegie said, "Millionaires rarely smile." This is substantially true.[1]

Real wealth isn't found in what we acquire. As nineteenth-century slavery abolitionist and clergyman Henry Ward Beecher asserted, "In this world it is not what we take up, but what we give up, that makes us rich."

"IN THIS WORLD IT IS NOT WHAT WE TAKE UP, BUT WHAT WE GIVE UP, THAT MAKES US RICH."—HENRY WARD BEECHER

NOT FOOL'S GOLD

I believe there is a wealth that is greater than money, and it comes from how you interact with others. People who practice the Golden Rule treat others with dignity and respect and can be content in the knowledge that they are living an ethical life. However, it's possible to take the Golden Rule to another level. You can develop a "Midas touch" *with people* by taking your focus off yourself and what you can gain, and instead focusing on adding value to others.

YOU CAN DEVELOP A "MIDAS TOUCH" WITH PEOPLE BY TAKING YOUR FOCUS OFF YOURSELF AND WHAT YOU CAN GAIN, AND INSTEAD FOCUSING ON ADDING VALUE TO OTHERS.

Giving truly is the highest level of living. It makes the world a better place. And it also makes for better business. H. E. Steiner asserted, "We shall have better business when everyone realizes that while it pays to invest money in their industries and develop natural resources, it pays still higher dividends to improve mankind and develop human resources." If you desire more than just a full bank account and you desire to build real riches—by investing in people— then strive to live out the following practices:

1. Treat People Better Than They Treat You

It's easy to love people who love you. And showing kindness to people who treat you well is little more than common courtesy. But how do you respond to poor treatment by others? Do you return disrespect with disrespect? Do you meet aggression with aggression? It doesn't take much for unkindness to escalate into greater conflict. Take a look at some of these seemingly petty disagreements that grew into full-blown war:

- A dispute between the cities of Modena and Bologna over a well bucket about nine hundred years ago began a war that devastated Europe.
- A Chinese emperor once went to war over the breaking of a teapot.
- Sweden and Poland flew at each other's throats in 1654 because the king of Sweden discovered that his name in an official dispatch was followed by only two *et ceteras,* while the king of Poland had three.
- The spilling of a glass of water on the Marquis de Torey led to war between France and England.
- By throwing a pebble at the Duc de Guise, a small boy caused the massacre of Vassy and the Thirty Years' War.[2]

It takes a person of strong character to treat others better than they treat you! As civil rights leader Martin Luther King Jr. said, "Forgiveness is not an occasional act; it is a permanent attitude." If everyone practiced the Golden Rule, the world would be a better place. But think about what kind

"FORGIVENESS IS NOT AN OCCASIONAL ACT; IT IS A PERMANENT ATTITUDE."—MARTIN LUTHER KING JR.

of world it would be if everyone strove to treat others *better* than they are treated. I call that living by the Platinum Rule.

My father taught me to take the high road in my treatment of others, even when they take the low road in their treatment of me. My father was a college president, and I remember a faculty member asking him what he thought about a man who lived in our community. My father said, "I think he's a fine man."

"Well, you should hear what he says about you," the faculty member said, and he went on to describe what the man had said about my father. "What do you have to say about him now?" the faculty member pressed.

"I've already told you," my father answered, "I think he's a fine man."

"Even after what he said about you?"

"You asked me what I thought of him," said my father, "not what he thought of me."

I've worked my whole life to follow my father's modeling, though I'm not as good as he was at practicing the Platinum Rule. I try to treat everyone I meet with respect. I desire to be a giver in every relationship. I can honestly say that I have no enemies. If I have an issue with somebody, I address it as soon as I can; then I move on. And I hold no grudges. They only get heavier the longer you carry them.

Try taking the high road with people, even when they don't treat you with the respect you feel you deserve. Try to *be kind* instead of treating people *in kind*. You'll find that it's very freeing.

2. Walk the Second Mile

There's an old joke I used to tell at leadership conferences that goes like this:

Here are some absolutely irrefutable statistics that show exactly why you are tired. There aren't nearly as many people actually working as you may have thought, at least not according to this survey.

- The population of this country is a little over 250,000,000.
- 84,000,000 people are over 64 years of age and retired. That leaves 166,000,000 of us to do all the work.
- People under 20 years of age total 95,000,000—so that leaves 71,000,000 to do the work.
- There are 27,000,000 who are employed by the government, which leaves 44,000,000 to do the work.
- 14,000,000 are in the armed forces, which leaves 30,000,000 to do all the other work.
- Deduct 20,000,000—the number in state and city offices. That leaves 10,000,000 to do the work.
- There are 6,000,000 in hospitals, mental institutions, and various asylums, so that leaves 4,000,000 to do the work.

- Now it may interest you to know that there are 3,999,998 people in jails and prisons—so that leaves just 2 people to carry the load.

That's you and me—and I'm about ready for a vacation![3]

The joke may be corny, but it contains a seed of truth. There seem to be a lot of people in this world who aren't doing their fair share of the work.

People who do the bare minimum never achieve much in life—for themselves or for others. Television host Oprah Winfrey says, "Doing my best at this present moment puts me in the best place for the next moment." I agree with that wholeheartedly. That's true not only in your work, but also when it comes to personal relationships. That's why I suggest that a person walk the second mile. I'll describe what I mean by explaining where the expression comes from.

Two millennia ago in the Roman Empire, a Roman officer could compel anyone to carry a load one mile. It was the officer's right, and a person refused at his peril. So to walk the first mile was to do what was required. I'm recommending you not only do that, but strive to go above and beyond that. See the extra mile as an opportunity to make a positive impact on the lives of others, to add value to people.

A person with an extra-mile attitude is someone who:

"DOING MY BEST AT THIS PRESENT MOMENT PUTS ME IN THE BEST PLACE FOR THE NEXT MOMENT."—OPRAH WINFREY

- Cares more than others think is wise.
- Risks more than others think is safe.
- Dreams more than others think is practical.
- Expects more than others think is possible.
- Works more than others think is necessary.

As my friend Zig Ziglar says, "There's no traffic jam on the extra mile." If you always do more than is expected, not only will you rise up above the crowd, you will help others to rise up with you.

"THERE'S NO TRAFFIC JAM ON THE EXTRA MILE."
—ZIG ZIGLAR

---

3. Help People Who Can't Help You

We live in a competitive culture. Businesses are positioned to crush their competitors. Sports teams look for any weakness in their competition so they can exploit it in order to win. Even reality TV shows pit people against each other to see who will become the ultimate survivor. Often we define our success by how much better we are than the next person. And when we do help others, we insist that it be a win for us as well. Let's face it: We don't often think like writer John Bunyan, who said, "You have not lived today successfully unless you've done something for someone who can never repay you." Yet if we want to live at the highest level, that's what we must do.

One of my favorite examples of that kind of help occurred

during the Winter Olympics in 1964. Back then, the greatest bobsledder of all time, Italy's Eugenio Monti, was engaged in the two-man bobsled competition. The Italian team had a good time during their first run. So did the British team, whose driver was Tony Nash. Following Monti's second run, he was in first place. And it looked as if he and his team-mate might win the gold medal as long as the Brits didn't surpass them.

As the British team prepared for their second and final run, they made a demoralizing discovery. During the first run, a bolt had broken on their rear axle, and they didn't have a replacement. They had no choice but to drop out. But Eugenio Monti, who was waiting at the bottom of the hill to see if his time would hold up, heard about what had happened to the British team. He removed a bolt from the rear axle of his own sled and sent it up the hill to his competitor. Nash's team used the bolt, made their run, and won the gold medal. Monti and his teammate ultimately finished in third place.

There was no way that Nash could repay Monti. And there was no way Monti could benefit from giving Nash the bolt. Yet he did it anyway. The criticism against Monti in the Italian press was scathing. But he let everyone know that he wanted to win *only* if he truly was the best. "Tony Nash did not win because I gave him a bolt," explained Monti. "Tony Nash won because he was the best driver."[4]

"YOU HAVE NOT LIVED TODAY SUCCESSFULLY UNLESS YOU'VE DONE SOMETHING FOR SOMEONE WHO CAN NEVER REPAY YOU."—JOHN BUNYAN

If you want to help people, then embrace the motto of nineteenth-century evangelist D. L. Moody, who advised:

> Do all the good you can
> To all the people you can
> In all the ways you can
> For as long as you can.

And when you can do that for people who can't do anything for you in return, then you're really developing the Midas touch, because you are adding value to the lives of others.

4. Do Right When It's Natural to Do Wrong

If you're over age thirty, then I'm sure you remember the Cold War between the U.S. and the Soviet Union. For more than three decades, the relationship between the two governments was characterized by mistrust and hostility. When Ronald Reagan became president of the United States, he determined that he wanted to change the interaction between the two superpowers. His first step was to write a personal letter to Leonid Brezhnev, the Soviet premier, asking that they try to "find lasting peace." To say that Reagan's overture got a cold reception would be putting it mildly.

It would have been natural for Reagan to give up trying to improve Soviet relations. He wouldn't have been the first president to do so. But he persevered. And eventually the ice melted and the Iron Curtain fell. Reagan's speech writer, Peggy Noonan, summed it up this way: "When you're strong, you can be 'weak.' When you know you are strong, you can trust yourself to make the first move, the first appeal, a request or a plea. . . . But when you fear you are weak or fear the world thinks you are weak, you are more inclined to make a great show of being 'strong,' and never write a personal letter asking for peace."[5]

It's not easy to do right when doing wrong is easier. It takes strong character. But the rewards can be remarkable, as they were for Reagan. That doesn't mean there is always a reward, because there isn't. But if you do wrong instead of right, there *cannot* be a good reward.

5. Keep Your Promises Even When It Hurts

Charles Brewer, the founder of MindSpring Enterprises, has made promise keeping foundational to his company. When MindSpring was founded in 1993, he included this statement in the company's core values: "We make commitments with care, and then live up to them. In all things, we do what we say we are going to do." He believed that if he could create a business environment where keeping promises was the norm rather than the exception, he would be significantly ahead of the competition.[6]

Brewer is certainly *different* from the competition. A

"WE MAKE COMMITMENTS WITH CARE, AND THEN LIVE UP TO THEM. IN ALL THINGS, WE DO WHAT WE SAY WE ARE GOING TO DO."—CHARLES BREWER study conducted by Dr. Pat Lynch was recently published in the *Journal of Business Ethics*. Lynch asked more than seven hundred businesspeople and graduate business students to rank their values in the workplace. Included in addition to promise keeping were items such as competency, work ethic, seniority, and overcoming adversity. Lynch found that keeping promises was at the bottom of people's lists. That held true in the survey regardless of gender, supervisory experience, or religious background.[7]

The irony is that promise keeping is the cornerstone of all relationships, and it is absolutely essential for success in business. Joseph Abruzzese, president of sales for CBS Television, observes, "In selling commercial time, integrity means everything. About 80 percent of your business comes from the same people every year, so selling is about the strength of the relationships. In the end, the honest broker really does win."[8]

Where do you draw the line when it comes to keeping a promise? You probably have no trouble keeping one when it's convenient. How about when it isn't? What about when keeping it will really hurt? That's what Sir Walter Scott did. You may be familiar with Scott. A biographer, critic, historian, and poet, Scott is considered the father of the historical novel, and he is credited with influencing novelists Leo Tolstoy, Alexandre Dumas, Victor Hugo, Honoré de Balzac, and others.

Scott was born in 1771 in Edinburgh, Scotland. He began his professional life as a lawyer following an apprenticeship under his father, but he soon turned to writing and quickly became the most popular novelist of his day. In 1808, he became a partner in a publishing company, which yielded him greater revenue than simply placing his works with another publisher. In 1826, his publishing company found itself in financial trouble when it was caught up in another business's bankruptcy. The debt was enormous: £114,000. Scott probably could have avoided the responsibility for paying the debt by declaring bankruptcy, but he didn't. Instead, he agreed to pay it all off.

Over the next six years, Scott, an already prolific author, wrote mountains of pages to earn money. He sold copyrights. He did whatever he could. In the end, he raised £70,000—before he died. Some believe he wrote himself to death. But his will gave instructions concerning how additional works could be sold, and the entire debt was paid. Not only did he not allow pain to stop him from keeping a promise, he would not allow even death to do it.

You don't meet many people like Scott today. Most of us prefer to do what's easy instead of what's right. But if we really want to live a golden life, then we would do well to follow his example.

THE GOLD STANDARD

Where are you currently focusing your attention? Are you trying to build a golden life? What opportunities are you currently pursuing? If you were to seize them, what rewards would they bring? Wealth? Promotion? Recognition? Awards? Let's put them in perspective. Take this quiz:

1. Name the five wealthiest people in the world.
2. Name the last five Heisman trophy winners.
3. Name the last five winners of the Miss America contest.
4. Name ten people who have won the Nobel prize.
5. Name the last half dozen Academy Award winners for best actor and actress.
6. Name the last decade's World Series winners.

How well did you do? How many names did you know? Half? Seventy-five percent? These people and teams—the best in the world at what they do—have accomplished much. They have proved that they have the magic touch in their area of expertise, and they have achieved great recognition. But what kind of impact have they made? More specifically, how much impact have they had on you? (Obviously not much if you can't even remember most of their names.)

Now, I want you to take another quiz:

1. Name three teachers who inspired you to achieve in school.
2. Name three friends who helped you through a difficult time.
3. Name five people who taught you something worthwhile.
4. Name three people who made you feel appreciated and special.

5. Name five people with whom you enjoy spending time.
6. Name half a dozen heroes whose stories have inspired you.[9]

You may not have scored 100 percent on the second quiz either, but I'm sure your score was better than on the first one. Why? Because these are the people who had the Midas touch in your life! Adding value to you was important for them. They focused on others—not just on getting ahead financially. If you want to do something that will make an impact beyond your own life, then treat people better than they treat you, walk the extra mile, help people who cannot help you, do right when it's natural to do wrong, and keep your promises even when it hurts.

You can tell when people have the Midas touch with others because they create a legacy that outlives them. Recently my father-in-law, Clayton Porter, died. When my wife, Margaret, who was his oldest child, and I attended the funeral, she spoke about his life. Clayton had been a teacher, and he had taught thousands of kids over the years. But Margaret said that his most important students were she and her sisters. Clayton had instilled in them not only a strong moral and ethical foundation, but also a love and respect for people. And he had done it, not just by teaching it, but by living it out.

When Margaret finished speaking, there wasn't a dry eye in the place—because the room was filled with hundreds of people whom he had taught, whose lives he had changed for the better. It was a legacy he would have been proud of. It's a legacy you could be proud of too.

Conclusion

Go for the Gold(en) Rule

I WANT TO ASK YOU TWO FINAL QUESTIONS. FIRST, WHAT DO you want to achieve? In other words, what goals have you set for yourself? Where do you want your career to take you? What impact do you desire to make? It's good to think about such things because it helps to set the *direction* for your life. The second question is this: How do you plan to do it? That's important because it sets the *tone* for how you will live. And it also influences how you will end up.

I believe there are two basic paths to achievement a person can choose. You can go for the gold, or you can go for the Golden Rule. There are many people out there who have gone for the gold and who appear to have achieved all life has to offer. But appearances can sometimes be deceiving.

In 1923, a group of men met at the Edgewater Beach Hotel in Chicago. At the time, they were some of the wealthiest and most powerful people in the world. How wealthy? Together they controlled more money than was contained in the U.S. Treasury! They were captains of industry and political giants. They had gone for the gold—

and gotten it. Here is a list of their names, along with what became of them:

- Charles Schwab—president of the largest independent steel company—died broke.
- Arthur Cutten—greatest of the wheat speculators—died abroad, insolvent.
- Richard Witney—president of the New York Stock Exchange—died just after release from Sing Sing prison.
- Albert Fall—member of a U.S. president's cabinet—was pardoned from prison so he could die at home.
- Jess Livermore—greatest "bear" on Wall Street—committed suicide.
- Leon Fraser—president of the Bank of International Settlements—committed suicide.
- Ivar Kreuger—head of the world's greatest monopoly—committed suicide.[1]

Often people who go for the gold trade everything else of importance in their lives for the opportunity to gain it. But then they lose even those material gains. While short-term success may come to many people who put the acquisition of wealth first, you can best measure the quality of their lives by looking at their later years. Then it's much easier to see if they're a Clayton Porter or Mike Abrashoff, or if they're more like Dennis Kozlowski or Robert Torricelli.

There's a world of difference between people who go for the gold and those who go for the Golden Rule:

People Who Go for the Gold . . .	People Who Go for the Golden Rule . . .
Ask, "What can you do for me?"	Ask, "What can I do for you?"
Make convenient decisions.	Make character decisions.
Sacrifice family for finances.	Sacrifice finances for family.
Develop a rationale for their actions.	Develop relationships with their actions.
Possess a "me first" mind-set.	Possess an "others first" mind-set.
Count their dollars.	Count their friends.
Base their values on their worth.	Base their worth on their values.

When you meet someone who has continually chosen to go for the Golden Rule, you can sense it in the way that person treats people and how they live their lives. That was true when I met Howard Bowen, who has since become a good friend. Howard was responsible for the construction of many Kmart stores when the department store chain was at the height of its success. And it made him highly successful.

That road hasn't always been easy. When Howard was

I BELIEVE THERE ARE TWO BASIC PATHS TO ACHIEVEMENT A PERSON CAN CHOOSE. YOU CAN GO FOR THE GOLD, OR YOU CAN GO FOR THE GOLDEN RULE.

working on landing the first contract with Kmart, he went down to Florida to look at sites. After touring the area all day with two representatives from the corporation, one of the executives, who had a bad reputation, suggested that all of them go to a strip club. Now Howard had a dilemma. The deal he was trying to win was worth $40 million. And he knew that if he didn't go along with this man's request, he could jeopardize winning the contract. But Howard believed in practicing the Golden Rule, and he knew that going to a strip club would be a betrayal to his wife.

Howard summoned all his courage and asked to be taken back to the hotel before the group went out that night. "I'm sorry, but I just can't do it," he told them. "Besides, I really need some rest."

As they pulled up to the hotel's entrance, Howard got out of the van. That's when another one of the people who had been riding with them said, "You know, I really need to get some rest too," and he also got out of the van. Then another did. In the end, nobody went out that night. Later, the executive who had originally made the suggestion told Howard, "You have no idea how much I respect you." He also awarded Howard the contract. Is a person who maintains his integrity always rewarded in that way? Of course not. But what if Howard had compromised his ethics and still not won the contract? Then he would have had neither the revenue nor his self-respect.

Howard had to make many tough decisions early in his career, such as the time a steel subcontractor on a job asked to be paid before he had finished the work because of cash-flow problems. Often that's a risky thing to do. But

Howard asked himself, "How would I like to be treated in this situation?" He decided it was the right thing to do, and he paid the contractor. Over the years, the two men ended up doing a lot of work together.

What's interesting is that about a decade later, Howard was building his home, and he needed some steelwork done on the structure. It was during a time when business was booming, and nobody wanted to stop working on lucrative projects to do a small job like Howard's house. But his old contractor friend immediately put other work on hold to help Howard. And he told Howard why: "Do you remember the first job I did for you? You helped me out when I had cash-flow problems. I'll never forget that. I'm grateful that I can do something to help you."

Howard hadn't thought about that in ten years. At the time, he was simply doing what was right. But that's the wonderful thing about living according to the Golden Rule. You see, if people who go for the gold are very lucky, they get some gold. But those who go for the Golden Rule not only have a chance to achieve monetary wealth, but also to receive other benefits that money can't provide. People who live by the Golden Rule give themselves a chance to have it all!

NOTES

Chapter 1: Whatever Happened to Business Ethics?

1. "World-Class Scandal at WorldCom," www.cbsnews.com, 26 June 2002.

2. Roger Rosenblatt, "When the Hero Takes a Fall," *Time,* 21 January 2002, 130.

3. Richard Lacayo, "A Sport on Thin Ice," *Time,* 25 February 2002, 26.

4. "Americans Speak: Enron, WorldCom and Others Are Result of Inadequate Moral Training by Families," 22 July 2002, Barna Research Online, www.barna.org.

5. John C. Knapp, "Why Business Ethics Is Worthy of Discussion," *Atlanta Business Chronicle,* 18 November 2002, http://atlanta.bizjournals.com/atlanta.

6. Joseph Fletcher, *Situation Ethics: The New Morality* (Philadelphia: Westminster, 1966).

7. Executive Leadership Foundation, Inc., *Absolute Ethics: A Proven System of True Profitability* (Tucker, Ga., 1987), 22–23.

8. Quoted in *World Magazine,* 7 September 2002, 14.

9. Joie A. Gregor, "Focus on: The Chief Executive Officer" (Special Advertising Feature), *BusinessWeek,* 23 September 2002, 30.

10. Jeff Siegel, "Ethical Dilemma," *American Way,* 15 September 2002, 54.

11. Joan Ryan, "Corporations Need Honorable Leaders, Not

Remedial Ethics," *Atlanta Journal-Constitution,* 10 November 2002.

12. "Are You Guilty of Giving Your Employees an Ethical Flea Dip?", *Leading for Results,* www.ragan.com, 13 December 2002.

13. Linda Tischler, "Can Kevin Rollins Find the Soul of Dell?" *Fast Company,* November 2002, 112–14.

14. Lorraine Woellert, "You Mean Cheating Is Wrong?" *BusinessWeek,* 9 December 2002, 8.

15. John D. Copeland, *Business Ethics: Three Critical Truths,* quoted by Scimitar Ridge, LLC, 22 July 2002.

16. Executive Leadership Foundation, Inc, *Absolute Ethics,* 24.

17. Proverbs 4:18–19, *The Message.*

Chapter 2: Why This Rule Is Golden

1. "Honesty," in *The Forbes Book of Business Quotations,* Ted Goodman, ed. (New York: Black Dog and Leventhal, 1997), 408.

2. Matthew 7:12.

3. *The Traditions of Mohammed,* quoted at www.the-goldenrule.net, 23 September 2002.

4. *Talmud,* Shabbat 31a, quoted in "The Universality of the Golden Rule in World Religions," www.teaching-values.com, 23 September 2002.

5. Udana-Varga 5, 1, quoted in ibid.

6. Mahabharata 5, 1517, quoted in ibid.

7. Shast-na-shayast 13:29, quoted at www.thegoldenrule.net, 23 September 2002.

8. Analects 15:23, quoted at ibid.

9. Epistle to the Son of the Wolf, 30, quoted at www.fragrant.demon.co.uk/golden, 23 September 2002.

10. Sutrakritanga 1.11.33, quoted at ibid.

11. Ibid.

12. The Josephson Insititute, "What Is Ethics Anyway?" www.josephsoninstitute.org, 24 September 2002.

13. Quoted in Bob Benson, *He Speaks Softly: Learning to Hear God's Voice* (Waco, Tex.: Word, 1987).

14. Vice Fund Prospectus, www.vicefund.com, 21 January 2003.

15. Bob Smietana, "A Penchant for 'Sin,' " *Atlanta Journal-Constitution,* 7 December 2002, B2.

16. "Corporate Profile," www.synovus.com, 27 January 2003.

17. Interview with the author, 10 December 2002.

18. Tom Barry, "Bank Shot," *Business to Business,* September 2002, 46.

19. Interview with the author, 10 December 2002.

20. Dave DeWitte, "Georgia's Synovus Corp. Shows How to Be a Top Employer," *Pulse,* 16 June 1999.

Chapter 3: The Golden Rule Begins with You

1. Zig Ziglar, letter to author, 15 April 2002.

2. Ned Herrmann, *The Whole Brain Business Book* (New York: McGraw-Hill), 1996.

3. Christopher Caggiano, "Employment Guaranteed, for Life," *Inc.,* 10 December 2002, 74.

4. Source unknown.

5. Charles W. Christian, "10 Rules for Respect," *Leadership Journal,* Summer 1999, www.christianitytoday.com.

6. Cara Cannella, "Keeping It Flexible," *Inc.,* 10 December 2002, 76.

7. "A Profession Is Born: 1930s," Our History, McKinsey & Company, www.mckinsey.com, 10 February 2003.

8. John A. Byrne, "Goodbye to an Ethicist," *BusinessWeek,* 10 February 2003, 38.

9. Tammy Joyner, "HomeBanc Taps Minister as Corporate Conscience," *Atlanta Journal-Constitution,* 4 December 2002, www.ajc.com.

Chapter 4: Living a 24-Karat-Gold Life

1. "Georgia Coach Takes the Blame for Bad Call," *Augusta Chronicle,* 14 November 2001, www.augustachronicle.com.

2. Josh Kendall, "Richt Finding His Way," *Athens Daily News,* 18 March 2001, www.onlineathens.com.

3. "Fast Talk: Carole Black," *Fast Company,* December 2002, 72.

4. J. C. Penney, *Fifty Years with the Golden Rule* (New York: Harper and Brothers, 1950), 16.

5. Norman Beasley, *Main Street Merchant* (New York: Bantam, 1950), 63.

6. Penney, *Fifty Years with the Golden Rule,* 52.

7. Ibid.

8. Thomas Addington and Stephen Graves, *A Case for Character: Authentic Living in Your Workplace* (Nashville: Broadman and Holman, 1998), 12.

Chapter 5: Five Factors That Can "Tarnish" the Golden Rule

1. Steve Wilstein, "Doing the Right Thing Is More Important than Winning," 19 November 2002, www.yorknewstimes.com/stories, 17 April 2003.

2. Marie Brenner, "The Enron Wars," www.mariebrenner.com/articles, 11 February 2002.

3. Catherine Valenti, "Ethical Culture," abcnews.com, 20 February 2002.

4. M. Scott Peck, *The Road Less Traveled* (New York: Touchstone, 1978), 66.

5. Robert Browning Hamilton, "Along the Road," cited in Edith P. Hazen, ed., *The Columbia Granger's Index to Poetry,* 10th edition, New York, Columbia University Press, 1993; 34.

6. Richard Foster, in *Reasons to Be Glad,* comp. by *Decision* magazine eds. (LaVergne, Tenn.: Spring Arbor Distributors, 1988).

7. Mark Lewis, "A Dwindling Band of Brothers," *Forbes,* 11 November 2002, www.forbes.com.

8. Harriet Rubin, "Power," *Fast Company,* November 2002, 68.

9. "Online Extra: The CEO as Thief: A Psychological Profile," www.businessweek.com, 23 December 2002.

10. Bruce Horovitz, "Scandals Grow Out of CEO's Warped Mind-set," *USA Today,* 11 October 2002, 2B.

11. Robert Greene, *The 48 Laws of Power* (New York: Viking Press, 1998), 16, 37.

12. Proverbs 16:18 NIV.

13. Proverbs 11:2 NIV.

14. Proverbs 13:10 NIV.

15. Proverbs 29:23 NIV.

16. C. S. Lewis, *Mere Christianity* (San Francisco: Harper San Francisco, 2001), 122.

17. Ezra Bowen, "Looking to Its Roots," *Time*, 25 May 1987, 26.

18. Peggy Noonan, *When Character Was King* (New York: Viking Press, 2001), 199.

19. Davin Seay, "Interview with Jim Collins," *Halftime,* 23.

Chapter 6: Seizing Your Golden Opportunity

1. C. S. Lewis, *Mere Christianity* (San Francisco: Harper San Francisco, 2001), 132.

2. "Starwood Hotels Survey," *Reader's Digest,* September 2002, 19.

3. Source unknown.

4. "Senate Ethics Committee Admonishes Torricelli," *USA Today,* 30 July 2002, www.usatoday.com.

5. "Sen. Torricelli Quits Race," www.newsmax.com, 21 November 2002.

6. Keith H. Hammonds, "Harry Kraemer's Moment of Truth," *Fast Company,* November 2002, 96.

7. Proverbs 22:7 NASB.

8. Foster, in *Absolute Ethics,* 18.

9. Wolf J. Rinke, *Winning Management: Six Fail-Safe Strategies for Building High-Performance Organizations* (Achievement Publishing, 1997).

10. Mike Abrashoff, *It's Your Ship: Management Techniques from the Best Damn Ship in the Navy* (New York: Warner, 2002).

11. Interview with author, 13 November 2002.

Chapter 7: How to Develop the "Midas Touch"

1. Ted Goodman, ed., *The Forbes Book of Business Quotations* (New York: Black Dog and Levental, 1997), 891.

2. Source unknown.

3. Source unknown.

4. "Eugenio Monti," www.olympic.org/uk/passion/humanity, 25 February 2003.

5. Noonan, *When Character Was King*, 221.

6. Ellwood F. Oakley III, "Promise-keeping Has Lost Its Importance as a Core Value," *Atlanta Business Chronicle,* 18 November 2002, www.atlantabusinesschronicle.com.

7. Oakley, "Promise-keeping Has Lost Its Importance as a Core Value."

8. "Joseph Abruzzese," *Fast Company,* November 2002, 62.

9. Source unknown.

Conclusion: Go for the Gold(en) Rule

1. Bill Rose, *New York Herald Tribune,* 8 November 1948.

About the Author

John C. Maxwell, known as America's expert on leadership, speaks in person to hundreds of thousands of people each year. He has communicated his leadership principles to Fortune 500 companies, the United States Military Academy at West Point, and sports organizations such as the NCAA, the NBA, and the NFL.

Maxwell is the founder of Injoy Stewardship Services, as well as several other organizations dedicated to helping people reach their leadership potential. He dedicates much of his time to training leaders worldwide through EQUIP, a non-profit organization. The *New York Times* bestselling author has written more than thirty books, including *Developing the Leader Within You*, *Today Matters,* and *The 21 Irrefutable Laws of Leadership*, which has sold more than one million copies.

A Leader with Character Attracts A Team!

Step 1 – Take the Character Quiz

Visit **www.Ethics101Book.com** and take the free quiz to assess your knowledge of character. Both the questions and your answers will give you a better realization of the role that character plays in leading others.

Step 2 – Take Advantage of a FREE Training Lesson

Complete your Character Quiz at www.Ethics101Book.com, then request your **FREE** training lesson *The Secrets of Making Good Decisions*. This lesson was specifically chosen from John C. Maxwell's **Maximum Impact® Monthly Mentoring Series** to help you reach a higher level in your leadership development.

The Secrets of Making Good Decisions is available online in streaming audio format for **FREE**, or if you would prefer to add this lesson to your personal training library, we can ship you a copy on either CD or audiocassette for a minimal shipping charge of $2.00.

Step 3 – Train Yourself and Your Team

Maximum Impact takes the negative feel out of teaching ethics in the program, *The Power of One Training Curriculum.* Ethics is not something you can force feed your employees or teach just to cover a legal liability; it is a personal choice, a way of life. Based on the book, *Ethics 101,* this training course shows how people can live with integrity by using the Golden Rule as their standard—regardless of religion, culture, or circumstances.

Step 4 – Maximize the Training

Leadership development begins with you, and is a process that is only complete when you develop the leaders around you. Be a river of wisdom and encouragement, not a reservoir!

Maximum Impact Training is cutting-edge leadership development that is unsurpassed in the industry today. Through this facilitator-driven course you and your team will be able to identify your leadership strengths, map a leadership action plan, and develop the essential skills necessary to lead. Bring one of our experts to your company or have someone certified to deliver it to your organization. Either way, you and your team will develop as leaders through this powerful training.

Step 5 – Train with a Proven Coach

John C. Maxwell tells us that leadership is developed daily, not in a day. You can grow your leadership on a daily basis by becoming a member of the **Maximum Impact Monthly Mentoring Club.** During your drive time, turn your car into a "leadership university" by listening to this powerful monthly resource. John will present relevant, insightful content to you each month in a CD or audiocassette format. Don't miss out on this dynamic growth tool.